CELEBRATING THE AMERICAN MUSICOLOGICAL SOCIETY AT SEVENTY-FIVE

American Musicological Society

The object of the Society shall be the advancement of research in the various fields of music as a branch of learning and scholarship.

Copyright © 2011 American Musicological Society, Inc.

Published by the American Musicological Society, Inc.
6010 College Station, Brunswick, Maine 04011-8451

www.ams-net.org

All rights reserved. No part of this publication may be reproduced, stored in a retrieval system, or transmitted, in any form or by any means, electronic, mechanical, photocopying, recording, or otherwise, without the prior permission of the American Musicological Society.

Library of Congress Control Number: 2011904502

ISBN 978-1-878528-14-9

Manufactured in the United States of America on acid-free paper.

Contents

Preface   5

Presidential Forum, Philadelphia, 2009

    Regard the Past, Examine the Present, and Look   13
toward the Future: The AMS at Seventy-five
        Jane A. Bernstein

    The AMS at Seventy-five: Some Personal Reflections   15
        Lewis Lockwood

    Let's Face the Music and Dance (or, Challenges to   25
Contemporary Musicology)
        Suzanne G. Cusick

    Enterprising Students and the Future of the   33
American Musicological Society
        Charles Hiroshi Garrett

An Anniversary Essay

    AMS 75: The American Musicological Society   45
Celebrates a Birthday
        James Haar

Documents from the AMS Archives   67

Appendices

    Society Officers and Board Members   83
    Honorary Members   93
    Corresponding Members   95
    Editors-in-Chief of the Journal of the American Musicological Society   97
    Annual Meetings   98
    Winners of Society Awards   100
    Research and Travel Grant Recipients   116
    Fellowship Recipients   119
    Books and Editions Published by the Society   123
    Music of the United States of America   126

Preface

GREETINGS! It is with great pleasure that I introduce this booklet celebrating the seventy-fifth anniversary of the American Musicological Society. Plans for a memento of our anniversary began several years ago, when the Committee on the History of the Society, chaired by Elizabeth Aubrey, proposed to the AMS Board the creation of a commemorative DVD. As our anniversary grew closer and time grew shorter, the Board decided that we should publish a booklet similar to the one issued during our fiftieth anniversary. At that time, Richard Crawford, then President of the AMS, wrote the superb essay "American Musicology Comes of Age: The Founding of the AMS," which traces the history of the Society up to 1950.[1] James Haar, who played an instrumental role in that publication, was invited to write the essay for this occasion. The present booklet was to be distributed at our Philadelphia meeting, but in light of the historic nature of our celebration, all agreed that we expand its scope and significance to include a commemoration of the meeting itself.

The seventy-fifth anniversary meeting was, by all accounts, a magnificent affair. Philadelphia, the site of our first and fiftieth anniversary meetings, offered the perfect setting for our grand fête. No fewer than 1,600 people were in attendance, representing all ages of the Society from undergraduate students, some of whom were there under the auspices of the Eileen Southern Cultural Diversity Fund, to long-term members of over sixty years. The program reflected the eclecticism of our discipline as did memorable evening musical events ranging from the Philadelphia Orchestra, Thomas Hampson's "Song of America" recital, and the contemporary music group, Orchestra 2001, to Jazz at the Painted Bride, and the early music group, Piffaro. Two new features of the meeting, "prime time" panel sessions by various AMS study groups and committees, and five mid-day concerts (three in a venue outside the hotel) proved to be a huge success.

The theme of past, present, and future permeated the meeting, not only with the amalgamation of new and old on the program, but also in the special events. A fascinating poster display of memorabilia in the book exhibit area, prepared by AMS Archivist Marjorie Hassen, celebrated the early years of our Society. Documents on display included nomination letters for membership of several illustrious musicologists, and Gustave Reese's 1936 letter to Otto Kinkeldey informing him about the newly constituted American Musicological Society. The *pièce de résistance*

---

1. Richard Crawford, "American Musicology Comes of Age: The Founding of the AMS," in *The American Musicological Society 1934–1984* (Philadelphia: American Musicological Society, 1984), 1–23.

was a souvenir program from the first International Congress hosted by the AMS in 1939 (see pp. 76–80). Held to coincide with the New York World's Fair, the congress featured the best American musicology had to offer, with sessions on Primitive and Folk Music in North America, Mediaeval and Renaissance Music, Music and Science, and Hispanic Music. Interestingly, the program of that early conference mirrored in many ways our present seventy-fifth anniversary meeting in its breadth and scope.

Paying homage to our history also dominated the Presidential Forum at the Philadelphia meeting, where we honored past presidents, honorary and corresponding members, and those who have held long-term membership in our Society of fifty years or more. The number of our esteemed members, many of whom made a special effort to attend, was extraordinary. Almost all our living past presidents, eighteen honorary members, and five corresponding members attended, as did over thirty of the nearly one hundred people who have been members for more than fifty years. Four of them—Edmund Bowles, Isabelle Cazeaux, Joseph Kerman, and Hans Tischler (who celebrated his ninety-fifth birthday in 2010)—were singled out in recognition of more than sixty years as AMS members.

Musicologists at the 1939 International Congress, New York.
Standing: Harold Spivacke, Otto Kinkeldey, Otto Gombosi, Knud Jeppesen, Fernando Liuzzi, Gustave Reese; Seated: Edward J. Dent, Carleton Sprague Smith, Curt Sachs, Alfred Einstein, Dayton C. Miller

Sixty-year AMS members in Philadelphia, standing, left to right: Joseph Kerman, Hans Tischler, Isabelle Cazeaux, Edmund Bowles

From recollections of the past, our thoughts shifted to the present at our Business Meeting and Awards Ceremony, where the *OPUS* Campaign took pride of place. The idea for this ambitious five-year capital campaign emerged at the March 2002 retreat of the Board in Columbus during Jessie Ann Owens's presidency. Elaine Sisman, then vice president, coined the campaign's acronym *OPUS:* Opening Paths to Unlimited Scholarship. The campaign was officially launched at a gala benefit dinner held at the 2004 AMS meeting in Seattle during Peter Burkholder's presidential administration. Jessie Ann Owens chaired *OPUS* during its initial phase until November 2005, when D. Kern Holoman and Anne Walters Robertson took over as co-chairs. By February 2006, the campaign was approaching its first million. During the past four years, *OPUS* has garnered major grants from the National Endowment for the Humanities, the Andrew W. Mellon Foundation, and the Gladys Delmas Foundation as well as contributions from nearly half of our membership. We can be proud that at the close of the campaign the amount raised totaled over $2 million.

At this culmination of our five-year fund-raising efforts, we can now reflect on what we have accomplished. Through the generosity of so many friends and members of our Society, we now have over twenty different publication awards, subventions, and travel grants. Two of the funds were established through major gifts by Thomas Hampson and Margarita Hanson. Many pay tribute to current esteemed members of our Society: Claire Brook, Lewis Lockwood, Joseph Kerman, H. Colin Slim, Ruth Solie, and Robert Stevenson. Others honor the memory of cherished colleagues—James Anthony, Elizabeth Bartlet, Barry Brook, Lenore

Fifty-year members left to right, **back row:** James Pruett, Lilian Pruett, Clayton Henderson, Aubrey Garlington, Rembert Weakland, Cynthia Hoover, Colin Slim, Howard Smither, William Porter, Herbert Kellman, Leo Treitler, Frank D'Accone, Glenn Watkins, Michael Ochs; **front row:** Sabina Teller Ratner, Lewis Lockwood, James Haar, Claire Brook, Bruno Nettl, Bathia Churgin, Edmund Bowles, Lavern Wagner, Sandra Rosenblum, Joseph Kerman, Theodore Karp

Coral, John Daverio, H. Wiley Hitchcock, Donna Cardamone Jackson, Jan LaRue, Janet Levy, Claude Palisca, Martin Picker, Harold Powers, Eileen Southern, and Eugene Wolf—who will live on for generations through these funds and through the great achievement of the *OPUS* Campaign.

If the Business Meeting and Awards Ceremony highlighted the present, our last special event, the Saturday night Joint Alumni Reception, celebrated the future of our Society. Twenty-seven universities participated in the event. At 11 PM we marked the conclusion of the *OPUS* Campaign by holding the last raffle drawings, which included a volume from the *Mozart Operas in Facsimile* contributed by the Packard Humanities Institute, two sets contributed by Oxford University Press: Richard Taruskin's *Oxford History of Western Music*, the *Encyclopedia of Popular Music*, and the magnificent AMS quilt handcrafted by Mary Natvig, Annegret Fauser, Lydia Hamessley, and Honey Meconi. Our celebrations ended with the singing of "Happy Birthday" to our Society (see the photos, pp. 40–42).

The present volume commemorates this historic occasion by offering essays by Lewis Lockwood, Suzanne Cusick, and Charles Hiroshi Garrett delivered at the 13 November 2009 Presidential Forum, photographs taken at the event (pp. 38–39, 60–63), and selections from the AMS Archives displayed at the meeting. It also presents the anniversary essay by James Haar originally commissioned for the booklet as well as appendices containing complete listings of past boards of directors, honorary and corresponding members, editors-in-chiefs of the *Journal of the American Musicological Society*, annual meetings, Society award winners, fellowship recipients, and books published by the AMS.

I should like to take this opportunity to express my thanks to Charles Atkinson, past-president, who initiated the booklet. John Roberts, chair of the Committee on the History of the Society, was there from start to finish, generously overseeing compilation of the lists and providing editorial assistance. I am grateful to Craig A. Monson, who assisted in the editing. Thanks also go to Robert Judd for his expertise with the production of the volume. We hope that you will enjoy this booklet and find it a fitting tribute and meaningful memento of our seventy-fifth anniversary.

Jane A. Bernstein
President

Presidential Forum

Philadelphia, November 2009

Regard the Past, Examine the Present, and Look toward the Future: The AMS at Seventy-five

Jane A. Bernstein

AS I BEGAN to think about this forum and its charge to celebrate the seventy-fifth anniversary of our Society, the emblem of my alma mater the City College of New York came to mind. It portrays an allegorical female figure, the three "Provinces of Scholarship," whose three faces look in different directions; one turns left, another right, and the third gazes straight at us. The inscription *Respice, Adspice, Prospice* that frames her three aspects roughly translates: Regard the past, examine the present, and look toward the future. I believe that commemorating our Society's anniversary is a fitting time to contemplate this motto.

Presidential Forum speakers Jane A. Bernstein, Suzanne G. Cusick, Charles Hiroshi Garrett, and Lewis Lockwood

Over the past three-quarters of a century our Society has witnessed many remarkable changes. From its founding fifty-one members, the AMS has grown to 3,500 strong. Our membership has not only increased in size but also in diversity. Two years after its creation, our Society included twenty women within a membership of 145; women now make up about fifty percent of the AMS. During the last decade, we have also witnessed a growth in the ethnic diversity of our membership, and in the coming years, our Society's multiculturalism will certainly continue to broaden. Our scholarly interests have also become more wide-ranging over the past twenty-five years. As we continue to draw on our discipline's past traditions, we have branched out and opened up to an astounding array of new subjects and discourses in the study of music. Musicology, like the musical experience itself, is a dynamic ongoing process, very much in the present, yet indebted to the past, and continually moving towards the future. These are exciting times indeed!

Now I am pleased to introduce essays by Lewis Lockwood, Suzanne Cusick, and Charles Hiroshi Garrett, who, in addressing the themes of past, present, and future, will offer their personal views of our Society, its history, and their place within it.

The AMS at Seventy-five: Some Personal Reflections

Lewis Lockwood

> The past is never dead. It isn't even past.
>
> —William Faulkner, *Requiem for a Nun*

IN 1984 RICHARD CRAWFORD wrote a fiftieth-anniversary essay on the founding of the society. In closing Crawford summarized what he took to be the founders' legacy:

> internationalism, probity, seriousness of purpose, and a dedication to a standard of quality that, if not explicitly defined, is nevertheless presumed self-evident to qualified practitioners of the craft . . .[1]

Crawford detected in the Society "a tone of formality that . . . together with a preoccupation with the past, has encouraged those who do not share it to look elsewhere for scholarly companionship."[2] Of course he was referring to the formation of the societies for ethnomusicology and for music theory in the 1950s and 1970s, by scholars whose interests lay outside Western music history, the traditional main province of the AMS.

Twenty-five years later, what has become of that "tone of formality" and what has happened since 1984 to color and transform the landscape? How did the Society come to be what it is today, and what will its future be like? Since my crystal ball is

---

1. Richard Crawford, "American Musicology Comes of Age: The Founding of the AMS," in *The American Musicological Society 1934–1984* (Philadelphia: American Musicological Society, 1984), 19.

2. Ibid.

Celebrating the American Musicological Society at Seventy-five, pp. 15–24. Copyright © 2011 by the American Musicological Society, Inc. All rights reserved. Please direct all requests for permission to photocopy or reproduce article content through the American Musicological Society web site, www.ams-net.org/contact.php.

in the repair shop, since I'm one of three contributors today, and since I'm speaking as a senior citizen with a long memory, I'll take the liberty of focusing more on the past than the future and I will mingle personal reflections with as much historical objectivity as I can muster.

I belong to the generation whose teachers founded this Society or were among its earliest members. They left an indelible stamp on it and on us. As an undergraduate at Queens College New York in the early 1950s I was swept into the field by Edward Lowinsky, who had escaped Nazi Germany, had come to Queens from Black Mountain College, and had recently published his celebrated book, *Secret Chromatic Art in the Netherlands Motet* (1946). However controversial its central thesis about secret chromaticism, this book was a passionate and brilliant portrayal of double meaning in music and in the cultural history of the Renaissance. Lowinsky was a formidable presence. In his music history course he played motets by Gombert and Clemens non Papa at the piano, moving into and out of his favorite passages with unwritten chromatic modulations. More broadly, he was an excellent pianist and a superb musician, whose course on analysis had us writing weekly papers on the Well-Tempered Clavier and on Beethoven piano sonatas.

From Queens I went on to Princeton for graduate work, there encountering scholars of the stature of Oliver Strunk, Arthur Mendel, and as a visitor, Nino Pirrotta. Differently gifted as they all were, Strunk made the deepest impression. In part for his magisterial command of the vast territories and byways of every field of music history, modestly and quietly communicated in seminars and in his only book, his *Source Readings in Music History* of 1950, which many of you probably know from the revised edition edited by Leo Treitler in 1998. What Strunk conveyed as a teacher stemmed from his reserved character, his restraint and patience in dealing with issues, with people, and with controversies. Strunk published very little. His insights were revealed in his teaching and kept in his meticulously written notebooks (which are now at the American Academy in Rome). It was in Rome that a number of his former students convened a conference in his memory in 2002. The papers were later published in the little volume, *Remembering Oliver Strunk: Teacher and Scholar*,[3] and I'm drawing on my own paper for that meeting in some of these remarks today. As Joe Kerman put it in his essay for Strunk, "Oliver always got at the really important question in anything he was dealing with . . . he would deconstruct the most tangled situations into a bundle of points that seem so simply and inevitably germane . . . that one hardly noticed the creative analysis behind them."[4]

As a founding member of the AMS in 1934, Strunk was then a mainstay within a small community of like-minded scholars, and it is no surprise that he was tapped

---

3. Christina Huemer and Pierluigi Petrobelli, eds., *Remembering Oliver Strunk: Teacher and Scholar* (Hillsdale, N.Y.: Pendragon Press, 2005). It contains an introduction by Anthony Newcomb and essays (in this order) by Petrobelli, Kenneth Levy, Harold Powers, Leo Treitler, Philip Gossett, P. Marco Petta, Herbert Kellman, Joseph Kerman, John Bergsagel, P. Nilo Somma, Agostino Ziino, myself, Jessie Ann Owens, Friedrich Lippmann, Robert Bailey, and Paula Matthews.

4. Kerman, "Salience and Serendipity," in *Remembering Oliver Strunk*, 43.

to be Editor-in-chief of the first issue of *JAMS* in 1948. After the hibernation imposed by World War II, the Society was ready to re-establish itself in a stronger and more optimistic way than before, and the *Journal* was to be the primary carrier of this new spirit. That spirit is still embodied in its By-Laws, which tell us that "the object of the Society shall be the advancement of research in the various fields of music as a branch of learning and scholarship." I need not say that every element in this statement is freighted with meanings and connotations that are likely to resonate differently now than they did three generations ago, but for me they continue to carry weight in changing times—or maybe I should say, even in our changing times. One connotation, so clear then and perhaps still needing emphasis, was that the very idea of a scholarly discipline for music was for many outside intellectuals a questionable proposition. For most people in the general culture, music was—and is—immediate experience pure and simple; music was what one played, or sang, or heard in concerts or recordings. To many people the idea of knowing music in its inner dimensions, thinking about its structural or historical perspectives, even its poetics, seemed a far-off or imaginary activity. Perhaps for this reason, as Crawford put it, there was a tacit understanding in the beginning that musicology in America should have a large measure of seriousness of purpose. And as it turned out, this small band of serious scholars quietly, and without the slightest touch of sensationalism, changed the American culture. They made it possible for musicology to become an accepted scholarly discipline.

In retrospect it is clear that in 1948 Strunk designed the first issue of *JAMS* to embody as broad a program as anyone could imagine in those years.[5] As he put it in his editorial preface, the appearance of a formal Journal "marks a turning point in the history of the Society and gives concrete expression to the Society's confidence in its own stability and sense of purpose." The opening article was a tribute by Otto Kinkeldey to Johannes Wolf, a pioneering medievalist who had died in Germany a year earlier, in 1947. In 1935 the Nazis had driven Wolf into retirement from his post at the Berlin State Library, and he had lived since then on a barely adequate pension. Strunk was personally close to both men. As a student Strunk had dropped out of Cornell and played the piano in silent movies in Buffalo and Rochester, had come back to Cornell in the 1920s to take a course in musicology there with Kinkeldey, and then went off to Germany to study with this same Johannes Wolf, who had also been Kinkeldey's doctor-father in Berlin back in 1909.

So the first article in the first *JAMS* had a personal and a professional agenda. It was written by Strunk's American father-figure about his German one, and it was also a tribute by the first AMS President, Otto Kinkeldey, to an eminent German scholar. In both ways it signals the indebtedness of American musicology to German scholarship, to *Musikwissenschaft* as a discipline, a field of dreams that aspired to knowledge of and about music over a wide range of intellectual domains but with Western music history as its core enterprise.

---

5. Some of what follows is based on my "Oliver Strunk, the *L'homme armé* and American Musicology," in *Remembering Oliver Strunk, Teacher and Scholar*, 81–88.

JOURNAL OF THE
AMERICAN MUSICOLOGICAL SOCIETY

EDITORIAL BOARD

Oliver Strunk, *Editor-in-Chief*   Carl Parrish, *Business Manager*
Nathan Broder   Donald J. Grout
J. M. Coopersmith   Otto Kinkeldey
Alfred Einstein   M. D. Herter Norton
Curt Sachs

CONTENTS

An Editorial	3
JOHANNES WOLF (1869-1947) . . . . Otto Kinkeldey	5
ON CERTAIN MANUSCRIPTS OF MOZART'S, HITHERTO UNKNOWN OR RECENTLY RECOVERED . . . . Alfred Einstein	13
ON THE USE OF SCORES BY SIXTEENTH-CENTURY MUSICIANS . . . Edward Lowinsky	17
"HOT" RHYTHM IN NEGRO MUSIC . . . . . Richard A. Waterman	24
Reviews	
A Birthday Offering to C. E. . . . . . M. D. Herter Norton	38
Otto Erich Deutsch, *The Schubert Reader* . Kathi Meyer-Baer	39
Alfred Einstein, *Music in the Romantic Era* . Donald J. Grout	40
Joseph Hutter, *Hudební nástroje* . . . . Paul Nettl	42
Knud Jeppesen, *Die italienische Orgelmusik am Anfang des Cinquecento* . . . . Glen Haydon	43
Curt Sachs, *The Commonwealth of the Arts* . . John Gutman	44
Communications	47
Announcements	50
Reports, 1947	52
Officers and Committees, 1948	61

Published by the AMERICAN MUSICOLOGICAL SOCIETY at 14 Beacon Street, Boston, Mass.
Editorial Office, Princeton, New Jersey

JAMS 1/1, Spring 1948

The rest of the first issue tells a further story about breadth and scope. Its other articles are by Alfred Einstein on Mozart manuscripts; by Edward Lowinsky on sixteenth-century scores; and by Richard Waterman, on "'Hot' Rhythm in Negro Music." Waterman's title is symptomatic of the era, but what is interesting is that his material ranged from music of West Africa and Trinidad to Tin Pan Alley, including three examples from the song "It's Always You" by Johnny Burke and Jimmy Van Huesen, quoting arrangements by Jack Mason and Benny Goodman. Waterman, by the way, was among the founders of the Society for Ethnomusicology a few years later.

Accordingly, the first issue of *JAMS* was a lot more ecumenical than most people might think, and it also offered a set of book reviews by M. D. Herter Norton; Donald Grout; Kathi Meyer-Baer; Paul Nettl; Glen Haydon; and John Gutman. If anyone is wondering about freedom of speech or editorial control, a reading of Grout's review of Einstein's *Music in the Romantic Era* should settle it. Grout recognized Einstein's brilliance and eminence in many fields, but he found this book disappointing, said it showed signs of "exhaustion"; and indicted it for what seemed to be "a constant, and apparently intentional avoidance of any coming to real grips with the substance of the music itself."[6]

So the little world of American musicology in 1948 showed a clear impulse towards substantial breadth, and *JAMS* revealed that it was open to opposing viewpoints among professional practitioners. To say that the former tendency continued in *JAMS* over the next decades would be unfortunately untrue. Instead, the rise of a parallel American journal for ethnomusicology soon began to absorb the energies of scholars in non-Western and vernacular musics. And although the seminal reviews by Milton Babbitt in *JAMS* in the early 1950s signaled that analysis and analytical thinking could find a home in the AMS, this field too was about to grow exponentially and its proponents would soon create other publishing outlets that gave them more scope.

Quite obviously I'm offering nothing more than a tiny telescopic view of the early past, the AMS of the early decades. By now, more than half a century later, cultural and political changes have shaken the world around us, and how could they not have a powerful effect on this field of scholarship as they have on all others? I'm thinking of the political upheavals of the post-World War II era; of the cold war and its aftermath; of Vietnam, Iraq, and Afghanistan, of globalization and the volatile economy of our times. I'm thinking of the changes in communication that have come with the digital revolution and all its consequences; of the avalanches of information that fall upon us now at the mere touch of a computer key, of Google, Facebook, and Twitter. How long will it be before all our books and articles are transmitted electronically, before students, already working away at their laptops and iPhones, read everything on e-books just as they read older articles on *JSTOR*?

Beyond all this there are deeper issues in American political and social history that impinge on what members of this Society do and how they do it. I'm referring

---

6. *JAMS* 1 (1948): 41.

to the civil rights movement that brought race relations to the forefront of our collective consciousness and laid the basis for the political transformations that have led to the election of Barack Obama. I'm referring to the new awareness of class, gender, and multi-culturalism that have swept the American intellectual and social landscape, with powerful consequences for our educational institutions and thus for what teachers and scholars do. I'm thinking of the intellectual turmoil surrounding the rise of post-modernism, with its challenges to traditional modes of knowledge and credibility in all intellectual fields. In our domain this has clearly been reflected in recent times by the proponents of a critical musicology that centers on the political, ideological, and contextual dimensions of music, largely though not exclusively under the banner of the "New Musicology." As Treitler pointed out, there are obvious parallels with the "New Historicism" in literary studies, and comparable developments in history and in art history.[7] Reactions to these shock waves have been evident in volumes with familiar titles: "Musicology and Difference," "Women Making Music," "Rethinking Music," "Beyond Structural Listening," and many more. New questions are being asked about the ontology of music, about works and contexts both historical and diachronic, about the cultural and social meanings of music, and many more related topics. All you have to do is to look at the programs of recent major musicological meetings (including this one) to see that multiplicity is the order of the day. I have no doubt that this spreading will persist, now and into the foreseeable future.

And so our Society at seventy-five has changed from being what it once was—a small and reasonably coherent fraternity of like-minded scholars—to become an umbrella organization, a structure for the annual ingathering of many independent subgroups, small communities of scholars or critics (or, if some people refuse the dichotomy, scholar/critics). As if in an annual replay of the California gold rush—and not without Chaplinesque moments—each group comes back to our national meetings to stake or renew its claim, carve out time and space, reinforce allegiances and create new ones, give papers or recitals and pursue discussions, draw up plans and ponder possibilities, launch newsletters and hang on for dear life to whatever financial support it can find. The term "interest group" can equally apply to those musicologists whose aim is to question the very nature of musicological discourse, thus of specialization itself as a condition of our intellectual and musical life.

Are we now witnessing an enlargement of what was, or a paradigm shift in the nature of the field and, accordingly, its principal American society? It depends on your point of view. Rose Rosengard Subotnik in a recent essay proposes what she calls a "Next Paradigm" for musicology, which she sees as "being shaped, in part, by doubts, and even a pervasive anxiety, about the status and future of writing.[8] On one level the question being raised is this: "in writing about music, what can

---

7. Treitler, "The Historiography of Music: Issues of Past and Present," in Nicholas Cook and Mark Everist, eds., *Rethinking Music* (Oxford: Oxford University Press, 1999), 356–77.

8. Subotnik, "Afterword," in Andrew Dell'Antonio, ed., *Beyond Structural Listening: Postmodern Modes of Hearing* (Berkeley: University of California Press, 2004), 280–302 and especially 285ff.

one say that is valuable and true?" She has much more to say about this than I can mention here, but the question is a profoundly important one.

In a time of intellectual ferment such as we have been living through for twenty-five years or more, there is a manifest tendency for dualistic thinking to dominate the discussion, in what I think is a misguided effort to express deeply complex tendencies and proclivities in simple ways: "Old" vs. "New;" "Historicist" vs. "Structuralist"—once upon a time, "History vs. Theory"—these are merely slogans of opposition that do little or nothing to reveal the subtle ways in which scholars actually think and work—and like all slogans they belong to parties that are designed to win followers. They make it uncomfortable for students to cross boundaries despite a wish to regain that sense of the wholeness of experience that they have been feeling about music since childhood. I can only voice my personal belief that no scholar I have ever known, however devoted to the deep pursuit of a special territory in a special field, has ever lost that underlying yearning to regain and express that sense of wholeness that makes the entire enterprise possible.

But I also want to raise a specter from the grave, namely old-fashioned specialization—which for me is not a limitation but a necessary condition for producing work that can have a chance to stand the test of time. In fact the claim for the value of specialization is as old as the serious study of scholarship itself. A classic statement of this view, if I may dredge it up from the deep, was Max Weber's essay of 1918, "Wissenschaft als Beruf," normally translated as "Science as a Vocation" even though the great sociologist meant by "Wissenschaft" not only the hard sciences but also the humanities, or humane sciences, as they are called in France. Weber was writing at a time of enormous historical change, his Germany having just collapsed at the end of World War I. In framing this essay he was well aware of the revolutions brought on by Einstein and by Freud, yet he also included the more traditional-minded humanities as part of his subject. Weber's primary plea was that anyone aspiring to scholarship accept the inevitable role of the specialist and have the unremitting intellectual curiosity that to Weber made true scholarship possible. Thus "whoever lacks the capacity to put on blinders, so to speak, and to come up to the idea that the fate of his soul depends on whether or not he makes the correct conjecture at this passage of this manuscript may as well stay away from science. He will never have what one may call the 'personal experience' of science."[9]

Now, so much has changed in the contours of intellectual life since Weber's time that we can hardly imagine that his concept of "science" or better, "Wissenschaft" can be simply transported into our time and milieu. For, although for many scholars of Western music history the fundamental importance of studying sources needs no underlining, we have to recognize that in many cultures in the world we live in, and in some dimensions of our own culture, "sources" are not only, or even mainly, written ones, but have to include unwritten forms of musical experience created by practitioners—composers, performers, musicians of every

---

9. Max Weber, "Science as a Vocation" (1918), often reprinted; e.g., in Max Weber, *Essays in Sociology*, ed. C. Wright Mills et al. (London: Routledge, 1991), 77–128.

kind. However differently realized, they form a matrix of material we cannot ever afford to ignore.[10]

At this point I want to reflect on two personal experiences. I have been working in Western music all my professional life—first as a young cellist, then in the Renaissance with which Lowinsky dazzled me a long time ago; more recently in the late eighteenth and early nineteenth centuries, above all on Beethoven. The close study of Beethoven's life, work, and significance was a field to which I introduced myself, almost with a feeling of necessity, though not without guidance from earlier teachers such as Elliot Forbes and Milton Babbitt. At Princeton in the 1950s I had a seminar with Forbes on his revision of Thayer's classic biography; and it was from Babbitt, who then taught an astonishing survey of the history of theory, that I first heard the name of Gustav Nottebohm, the pioneering scholar of Beethoven's sketchbooks, whose work is still essential.

Two years ago I had occasion for the first time in my life to visit Bali, that extraordinary island now part of Indonesia, formerly a kingdom with a long and remarkable history. Bali is an island with about three million people and twenty thousand Hindu-Animist temples (within predominantly Muslim Indonesia it maintains a highly independent religious orientation.) I learned that in each temple and each service a group of men in temple garb play the gamelan, the famous ensemble of tuned gongs and other indigenous instruments. Since in each village in the country a religious service is practiced somewhere every day of the year, the sound of gamelan playing is everywhere. What I'm describing is obviously not a seasoned experience, it is just my limited impression as a novice visitor, a tourist, but it was enough to make me realize how true it is that such beautiful traditional music—whose "sources" are the people themselves who practice it—is entirely embedded in the fabric of social and religious life that has dominated this island for centuries.[11] Of course I have tried to find out more about this remarkable tradition, and I have learned a great deal from the writings of Colin McPhee and Michael Tenzer, who have devoted their lives to the elucidation of this music and this culture.

And this experience made me think about "embeddedness" in the Western music that I have been involved with for so many years. When I worked with the Juilliard String Quartet on a recent book about selected Beethoven quartets, I was deeply aware at every moment that both they and I were totally immersed in these works, though with different yet overlapping, angles of vision. I was as deeply interested in their ideas on these quartets, as they painstakingly prepared their performances and annotated scores—as they were in finding out about what biography and source studies can show us, even in bare outline, about the origins

---

10. Again, this viewpoint was richly elaborated by Nino Pirrotta in his work on late medieval music, and more broadly as well as eloquently by Leo Treitler in many of his essays on music, history, and methodology.

11. My reading on the subject has led me to the work of Colin McPhee and to Michael Tenzer's *Balinese Music* (North Clarendon, VT: Charles Tuttle Co., 1998) and his other books on Balinese music, based on years of experience living in Bali and interacting with local musicians.

of these works. For example, about Beethoven's revision of Opus 18 No. 1, for which we have two complete versions; or about the drastic compositional changes he made as he was writing out the final version of Opus 59 No. 1.

Nobody doubts that to play as well as the Juilliard Quartet requires, to put it mildly, "specialization"—and yet all of us who are non-professional chamber music performers can aspire to such a level, whether we reach it or not. Still, we also know that no one can do everything equally well. So do they when it comes to what musicologists know about the works we have studied for a lifetime—these performers regard such experience with the respect and pleasure that comes with gaining new perspectives on something you love. Above all there was a feeling of mutual engagement, and of humility in the face of our joint responsibility in dealing with works of the highest caliber, whose mysteries we were exploring.

This experience resonates with what Richard Rorty called "the inspirational value of great works of literature."[12] I'm not suggesting that such works cannot be, and should not be, studied in many other ways, including their wide ranges of possible meanings and contexts—but it does mean that in our field such wider dimensions take on greater significance the more they grow out of the deep engagement with musical substance that performing musicians take for granted. And if musicians like these are not clients for musicology, who is?

In the study of Western music history there is an undeniable focus not only on contexts but on individual composers from Perotin to Golijov and what they have tried to achieve, about the nature of popular and high art music through the ages, about musical experience, about style and substance, about organizing principles such as modality and tonality, about the origins and development of the music that is part and parcel of our history and culture—that is, we or some of us as Americans who stem from European roots. Some of the questions we ask can also resonate with those of other cultures, and even subcultures within our own larger framework—but when we study works of high art music created by master composers of the past, by Josquin, Mozart, or Wagner—quite obviously a host of issues will arise that do not normally appear in the study of cultures far removed from our own. I'm well aware that every element in what I have just said is the subject of ongoing cultural and historiographic critique by various scholars, and in the few brush-strokes of this brief contribution I can hardly get deeply into them. But what it reflects is the plurality of musics, therefore of musicologies, and of the importance of keeping a healthy respect alive for what other people do that is different from what you do.

In closing I'll just invoke an ancient and homely parable, that of the ship of Theseus. According to Plutarch, the hero Theseus had a ship that was preserved in Athens long after his time. The legend is that the Athenians gradually removed the planks of the ship as they decayed, one by one, and put in new ones. So philosophers from then on asked this enduring question: since eventually none

---

12. Rorty, "The Inspirational Value of Great Works of Literature," in his *Achieving Our Country* (Cambridge, MA: Harvard University Press, 1998), 125–40.

of the planks were the original ones, was the later ship the same one that formerly belonged to Theseus?

This society is our ship but we are also its ship-builders. We have a collective obligation to keep it in as good repair as we can, both while we sail on it and when we replace its planks, which I believe we should do as carefully and judiciously as we can. It is a collectivity bound loosely together by common interests, yet without some effort to hold it together it could be torn apart by sectarian oppositions. What then will we do about difference?

If there is a message in all this, it comes down to a call for both passion and restraint, the qualities I ascribed earlier to my two most formative teachers, Lowinsky and Strunk. Passion and imagination in the pursuit of difficult questions; restraint and tolerance for diversity. It means reading and hearing papers in fields you know nothing about, written from angles of insight utterly unlike your own, to get the feel of what is going on in someone else's territory. It means a recognition that the tracks in the forest may well have been trodden by predecessors who have to be given their due; that knowledge is cumulative, not entirely invented anew with every discovery; that our ancestors are our colleagues, right now.

We live amid much controversy about methods, modes of discourse, about the nature of musicology and its objects of study. But at the end of the day what is going to hold the field together is some distant sense of shared purpose and a combination of passion and restraint that are both worthy of emulation. My hope for the future of the AMS is the same as my hopes for the field, that a latent sense of common purpose can keep this society flourishing even as its communities and interest groups multiply and expand and as it moves forward in changing times.

Let's Face the Music and Dance
(or, Challenges to Contemporary Musicology)

Suzanne Cusick

> *There may be trouble ahead*
> *But while there's moonlight and music*
> *And love and romance*
> *Let's face the music and dance.*[1]

STEEPED AS I AM in the tradition of musicology that values the long-term implications of origins, and that, as a result, inhabits a temporality in which past, present, and future are mysteriously intertwined, I begin by remembering that the American Musicological Society was born in a time of crisis. The United States' financial system was in ruins. Intellectuals of all political stripes struggled both to identify a "usable past" for the renewal of our country and to identify ways the arts could influence public life. Unemployment peaked in 1934, the year of our founding, at a staggering 21.7%. Yet troubled as it was, the time of our society's origin was also a time of great creativity and wit—a time when Irving Berlin, through the bodies of Ginger Rogers and Fred Astaire, taught the country to think of music, love, and romance, and then face the music and dance.

I.

Music. Love. Romance. I cannot think of these notions in relation to the society's origins without remembering the name of Ruth Crawford Seeger. As Judith Tick, Ellie Hisama and others have ensured we know, Ruth Crawford was in Blanche Walton's apartment on West 4th Street in New York when her future husband, Charles Seeger and other founding members of the parent organization of the

---

1. Irving Berlin, "Let's Face The Music And Dance," Copyright © 1935, 1936 by Irving Berlin; Copyright renewed. International copyright secured. All rights reserved. Reprinted by permission.

Celebrating the American Musicological Society at Seventy-five, pp. 25–32. Copyright © 2011 by the American Musicological Society, Inc. All rights reserved. Please direct all requests for permission to photocopy or reproduce article content through the American Musicological Society web site, www.ams-net.org/contact.php.

AMS, the New York Musicological Society, held their second meeting on February 22, 1930. As she wrote in her diary:

> The musicologists meet. It is decided that I may sit in the next room and hear [Joseph] Yasser about his new supra scale. Then when I come out for this purpose, I find someone has closed the doors . . . I walk past the closed door to my room, and when I pass I turn my head toward the closed door and quietly but forcibly say, "Damn you," then go on to my room and read Yasser's article. Later, my chair close to the door, I hear some of the discussion.[2]

Later still, in 1972, Charles Seeger would remember that he had excluded Crawford "to avoid the incipient criticism that musicology was 'women's work'."[3]

Crawford's exclusion at that meeting, I think, predicted the long-vexed relationship of our society to gender (that is, to masculinity, femininity, women, people of non-normative sexualities), to difference more generally, and to musical creativity. Yet today we celebrate our diamond jubilee under the leadership of a woman president, Jane Bernstein—and she is far from the first. Indeed, since Janet Knapp's election in 1975, and including Jane's successor, Anne Walters Robertson, the society will have had nine woman presidents (out of thirty-eight, so just under twenty-five percent of the total). I might add that it was a woman musicologist, Eileen Southern, who squarely addressed our profession's legacy of racial exclusions by writing the first survey text of African American music.[4] And although its first, 1970s wave dissipated all too soon—partly under pressure from a terrible job market—the second wave of feminist work in musicology has had significant effects on our society and our discipline, garnering one of our field's few MacArthur Fellowships for Susan McClary's brave, pioneering work; almost completely washing away our mid-twentieth century fetishizing of "the music itself," and leaving in its wake the effort to balance critical, historical, and analytical approaches that was dubbed, now twenty years ago, a "new musicology." Further, feminist musicologists succeeded in "changing the subject" (in Ruth Solie's memorable phrase) to allow musicological knowledge claims to be made from many subject positions that our founders excluded.[5] The profound queerness— the non-normativity, even the intrinsic, campy *fabulousness* and *fun*—of which

---

2. For more analysis of the incident's implications, see my "Gender, Musicology, and Feminism," in Nicolas Cooke and Mark Everist, eds., *Rethinking Music* (Oxford: Oxford University Press, 1999), 471–98. I first encountered the story in Ellie Hisama, "The Question of Climax in Ruth Crawford's String Quartet, Mvt. 3," in Elizabeth Marvin and Richard Hermann, eds., *Concert Music, Rock and Jazz since 1945: Essays and Analytical Studies*, Eastman Studies in Music, 2 (Rochester: University of Rochester Press, 1995), 285–312. See also Judith Tick's magisterial *Ruth Crawford Seeger: A Composer's Search for American Music* (Oxford: Oxford University Press, 1997), 121–22.

3. Hisama, 291.

4. Eileen Southern, *The Music of Black Americans* (New York: W. W. Norton, 1971).

5. Ruth Solie, "Approaches to the Discipline: Changing the Subject," *Current Musicology* 50 (1992): 55–65.

musicology is capable has been not only acknowledged but, in many quarters, embraced. Increasingly, we think, talk, and write as if music were not a thing, not an autonomous entity, but a relationship; or, as if it were, to paraphrase Guthrie P. Ramsey, the audible circulation of social energy.[6]

And yet, when I think of our present and our future, Ruth Crawford's and Eileen Southern's ghosts haunt me with questions. Are we really so much more comfortable than our grandparents with the gender liminality Anglophone cultures associate with musicality? Do we, now, let women, queers, "others" into our rooms, and on what terms? Tamara Levitz , the chair of this year's program committee, has noted the "distinct patriarchal frame" that persists in our own, collective submission of proposals for this epochal meeting, as she has noted our own lingering inclination to think of women as performers, not creators, and our lingering collective reluctance to submit to the Society's review our scholarly work on gender, sexuality, race and class.[7]

Do we, now, let active composers into the room, and, if so, on what terms? This very evening, we will have been able to hear Susan McClary interview a living composer, David Del Tredici. That special session, created and paid for by members of the society's LGBTQ Study Group, eerily re-split the roles of woman and creator that Ruth Crawford felt she had to straddle so long ago. At the same time, by staging the collegial exchange between a scholar and a creator that same session can seem to heal the 1930 exclusion of Crawford from the musicologists' room. Yet the multiply vexed relationships to alterity and creativity predicted by her exclusion may have been healed less ambivalently even earlier in the day, when scholar composers George Lewis and Nina Eidsheim addressed a special session on the musical aesthetics of race and ethnicity sponsored by the Committee on Cultural Diversity. In a jam-packed room, both spoke to the extent to which new music can constitute audible, somatically-enacted theorizing of the world—a kind of theorizing that illuminates the relationships it animates every bit as much as our mostly historical, sometimes interpretive or critical work.

Before the fiddlers have fled
Before they ask us to pay the bill
And while we still have the chance
Let's face the music and dance.

2.

I cannot think of our Society's present and future without seeing the pressing challenge that we engage anew the question of a usable past that so preoccupied

---

6. Guthrie P. Ramsey, Jr., *Race Music: Black Cultures from Bebop to Hip-Hop*, Music of the African Diaspora, 7 (Berkeley: University of California Press, 2004), 22.

7. Tamara Levitz, "AMS Philadelphia 2009 Program Selection," American Musicological Society web site. American Musicological Society, 1 November 2009; <http://www.ams-net.org/philadelphia/philadelphia-selection.php>.

intellectuals in the decade of our origin. Many of us work as teachers, one way or another, and therefore we are daily involved in identifying and sustaining "usable musical pasts." Like our grandparents, we might do well to ask ourselves "usable by whom, and for what interests?"

Our colleague Gary A. Tomlinson has suggested that all modern musicologies (including ethnomusicology) are entangled in a tradition of European culture that, sometime in the eighteenth century, arrogated to its own acoustical practices and mythologies the word "music," consigning the rest of the world's acoustical practices to such less transcendent notions as "song," "dance," "ritual." He further suggests that this notion of "music" helped to distinguish "the West" from "the rest" in the European imaginary.[8] Sustaining this distinction became the mostly unwitting work of our musicologies. Our music histories have done their part. In about fifty of this Society's seventy-five years, our music histories have provided the United States with a usable musical past that has sustained our nation's role as "leader of the free world" or, as people elsewhere might see it, as the successor and synthesizer of several European empires.

In the long decline of modernity that was the twentieth century, "music" thus defined has been gradually replaced as the de facto master discourse, in spite of (or perhaps because of) musicology's emergence as its main discursive support. Doesn't the use of music (or "sound design") to torture those who resist the United States' effort to sustain modernity's arrogation of world resources to the West represent the logical conclusion of the decay process? That is, doesn't the practice (so rooted in "modern" ideas of music's effect on the psyche) reveal starkly the violence embedded in this notion of "music" all along? At the same time, don't the prisoners' accounts of their bodies being battered by sound expose the utter non-ineffability of this "music" (and therefore, in a way, the utter non-transcendence of the culture that invented the construct)? And, doesn't it expose "the West" as having actually long acknowledged music as the opposite of ineffable, but as instead an almost irresistibly powerful medium of relationship that can all too easily turn into a real (not metaphorical or symbolic) weapon?

Soon
We'll be without the moon,
Humming a diff'rent tune,
And then

If the definition of "music" that our musicologies have sustained is in the last stages of its decay, then it seems likely that musicology may soon face a crisis more profound than either the minor revolution wrought by feminism and its offspring or the apparent employment crisis wrought by the current Great Recession. It will be more profound, too, than the need many of us recognize to reconfigure our

---

8. Gary A. Tomlinson, "Self, Other, and the Emergence of Musical Modernity," in *Music and Historical Critique: Selected Essays* (Aldershot and London: Ashgate, 2007), 189–96.

methodological and ideological relationships with ethnomusicology, music theory, "classical" new music, and that very new thing, "sound studies" (acoustemology).

With the collapse of modernity—through the last stages of which many of us will live—I think that what will be required of us is nothing less than a complete rethinking of what intellectual inquiry and speculation about music (and with music) might be, and of what kind of musical past might be usable in the new world taking shape. What purposes do we think music might, or should, serve? What should the generations that follow us know about the musical pasts to which we lay claim?

Do they need to learn that Francesca Caccini's musical career prospered because of her usefulness to a de facto regent? That Beethoven constructed a public image as a genius that stuck with his emerging bourgeois public to such an extent that the ideologies of heroism attached to that image would come to seem inscribed in the very notes of his scores, and in the sounds (ineffable or not) those notes imply?

What do they need to know about chant, or about sound and vocalization as dynamic forces in performing a relation to the sacred in twelfth-century Europe? What do they need to know about the influences of Arabic and Persian musical systems on European ones, or the mutual influence of indigenous and colonizing musics in the Americas, in Africa, in Asia? What do they need to know about the transformation of "music" in our time into something that might better be called "audible media?" What do we think people who aspire to lead marching bands or church choirs, or to play in classical orchestras, need to know? And what do we think the population at large needs to know about the acoustic as a register of human sensory/cognitive experience, so as to enable our fellow citizens to make informed decisions about acoustic manipulations in malls, by vendors of iPods and mp3 players, in hospitals, airports, and film theatres, and in our prisons? How can we best prepare future generations of musical creators, scholars, teachers, and citizens to respond to the educational, musical, and ethical needs of the United States' post-imperial moment, a moment we know is coming as surely as we know that global warming and the end of the world's petroleum reserves are.

There may be teardrops to shed.

3.

We cannot think well about the construction of a musical past usable for the challenges of this century without also acknowledging how shifts in our intellectual and educational missions will interact with shifts in the thing we loosely call "the job market." I was moved to do so some months ago. Reading the agony, disillusionment, anger, and despair on the AMS-list and the musicology wiki, expressed by young people who rightly feared for their economic and professional futures, I thought some one of us on this panel ought to respond. I thought it might as well be me, because I still remember what it felt like to lose a tenure-track job in 1982, when the Reagan recession drove the college where I worked into bankruptcy, and what it felt like to live for ten years the grindingly hard life of ad hoc, marginal and marginalizing labor as a journeyman adjunct faculty member, what it felt like to teach at three institutions in a single day, preparing lectures in my head as I drove from place to place.

But I do not want to patronize you, my un- and under-employed colleagues, nor do I want to slip into some patronizing, falsely empathetic stance, some version of "I feel your pain" or "just hang on!" I remember too well how similar remarks would fill me with rage when I was young. Rage, despair, envy; three of the seven deadly sins came close to choking me alive; only luck and the immense generosity of some senior scholars in this room saved me. What I do want to say to you is this: the seven deadly sins are called that because they kill your soul. If left unchallenged in your consciousness, they will destroy the best part of you, destroy the very gifts you have to share with the world. Nothing, not even music or musicology, is worth that. So I urge you to adopt whatever spiritual practice it might take to transform the energy of rage, despair, and envy into energy for good work that is part of a good life.

What I most want to say, however, is addressed to my tenure-track colleagues, especially those who are tenured and secure. Dear colleagues, our un- and under-employed colleagues are immensely gifted people who need our help. They need us to understand that they suffer not only from the economic contraction of the Great Recession, but also from a profound restructuring of the way people work in a new capitalism. This restructuring has been underway for thirty years.

As sociologist Richard Sennett and media scholar Marc Bousquet have elaborated at length, the paradigmatic enterprise of the new capitalism is designed to be flexible, responsive to market changes, rather than to be stable.[9] Responsiveness requires that an enterprise's workforce consist, as much as possible, of casual labor, easily hired and fired in response to economic change. Workers who value long-term relationships, long-practiced skills, long-developed depth of knowledge, the craft of doing a job well for its own sake are discredited if not dismissed. They are replaced by new workers, who seem endlessly flexible in their knowledges and skills, who operate best as independent contractors rather than as a members of a team, and who can reinvent or re-engineer themselves as circumstances demand. Both kinds of workers labor in environments that increasingly discourage institutional or interpersonal loyalty, trust among co-workers, and the kind of informal mentoring that develops from long-lived social relations with colleagues.

I suspect that many of us who are older hear in Sennett's description of the casualized workplace an explanation for what feels weird (or shallow, cold, presentist, unwelcoming) when we go to work. And I daresay all of us can hear, in the new capitalism's devaluing of depth and craft, a profound challenge to our foundational beliefs as musicians, teachers, and scholars (a challenge about which many of us feel increasingly threatened and uneasy). Yet, immersed as we are in ever-more frenetic lives of teaching, mentoring, research, and publishing that are,

---

9. Richard Sennett, *The Corrosion of Character: The Personal Consequences of Work in the New Capitalism* (New York: W. W. Norton, 1998), and Marc Bousquet, *How the University Works: Higher Education and the Low-Wage Nation* (New York: NYU Press, 2008).

nonetheless, lives of great privilege, many of us can forget that the forces that make us feel weird—about the jobs we are lucky enough to have, or about the changes and challenges in musicology and this society—are as much economic as they are substantively intellectual. Economic, and often in extremely distressing interaction with the traditions of exclusion based on alterity we thought we had, or could, overcome. Economic forces, that is, greatly exacerbate our anxieties about our discipline's inevitable shifts of style, substance, and subject, even as they lead us to wonder why we who have disciplinary privilege cannot effect more positive change.

We who work in academe, or aspire to do so, are all but locked into the system Sennett and Bousquet describe. The most obvious structural symptom of the new capitalism in our departments, and in our colleagues' lives, is the long-lived trend toward ever more opportunities for TAs, adjuncts, "visiting artists," post-doctoral fellows and non-tenure-track faculty on renewable contracts, and ever fewer entry-level tenure-track jobs, with ever higher standards for being hired, ever higher ones for tenure.[10] These very changes, I think, militate against our abilities to reinvent ourselves and our profession in response to new concerns (or in preparation for the new, post-imperial America that will surely come). Both the casualization of academic labor and the anxiety it produces put pressure on academic departments to maintain a curricular status quo. We who have found our way into the system have to produce published work to stay there, so we teach within pre-existing parameters (if often very innovatively) more than we might like to, "until the book is done." "The book" looms over us every day, discouraging us from the long lunches or relaxed drinks with colleagues in which the exchange of ideas and the team spirit to invent new curricula could be born. And, when we lose lines because of retirements or budget cuts, and must staff our core courses with adjuncts, we think, rightly, that it is irresponsible to put the burden of real curricular reform on our adjunct, temporary, post-docs, or three-year colleagues, many of them dismally paid and lacking benefits, or even on our tenure-track colleagues. How could we ask them to do other than step into the pre-ordained slots of the curricula they have inherited? The result is economically-based pressure to retain curricula that are structurally conservative, able only imperfectly to accommodate the hard-won new knowledges that have enabled our collective scholarly life to address (if not entirely resolve) the anxieties about alterity and creativity that vexed our society's origins, and utterly unable to accommodate the profound rethinking of our usable past that would prepare us and our fellow citizens for the trouble ahead.

This is a trap from which we must escape for the sake of our intellectual integrity, our respect for the best that has been part of our society's now-long tradition, and our commitment to the importance of scholarship about human acoustical

---

10. One of Bousquet's most valuable, if troubling, insights is his demonstration that those of us who form the increasingly small percentage of the academic labor force who are tenured faculty derive our privilege by *producing* this army of casual academic workers. They are our graduate students, our graduate programs' recent Ph.D.s. See Bousquet, 23, and Chapter Four, "Students Are Already Workers," 125–56.

experiences, human interventions in the acoustical environment. Although it is true that this Society cannot, as an institution, have any more impact on the labor practices of the new capitalism than it can on the acoustical practices of our government's dark prison at Kabul, we who are members of the Society can. I feel sure that we who are enmeshed in the academic part of the new capitalism can find ways to resist and evade the casualization of academic labor, the resulting exploitation of graduate students', adjuncts' and independent scholars' labor and erudition, and the resulting economic and social pressures on our discipline's capacity to change. We can do it even as we think about the relationship of our institutional and departmental labor practices to the political work our curricula contribute to sustaining an increasingly complex "American" identity (imperial or not) that engages its old anxieties about the relationship of gender, class, race, ethnicity, class, and culture to musical creativity.

We can do it because we come here—all of us—in love. Whether our notion of music is the one Tomlinson has identified or not, we are here to talk, think, make, write, be in the glorious presence of a medium and a relation and sometimes even, yes, a thing that we call "music" and that we just love, often with embarrassing and unaccountable passion. That passion is what circulates among us when we meet annually as a whole society, circulating most powerfully when it moves as social energy made audible—that is, as music. For many of us, it is a passion that has the force of the erotic, a force defined by the late Audre Lorde as the very medium of power. As she reminds us, "recognizing the power of the erotic within our lives can give us the energy to pursue genuine change within our world."[11]

"*So*," as Irving Berlin put it,

> *while there's moonlight and music*
> *And love and romance*
> *Let's face the music and dance.*

---

11. Audre Lorde, *Uses of the Erotic: The Erotic as Power* (Brooklyn: Out and Out Books, 1978), 8.

Enterprising Students and the Future of the American Musicological Society

Charles Hiroshi Garrett

WHEN I BEGAN preparing to talk about the past, present, and future of the AMS, I started down a familiar path. I went to the archives—reading publications about the Society and paging through the AMS newsletters stored on our Society's website. Some discoveries surprised me. For instance, in 1957, the AMS business meeting attracted a total of forty-eight members. At this year's conference we may have that many attendees from the Philadelphia metropolitan area alone. Here's another sign of change: in the first six decades of this Society, a total of three women were elected AMS President. In contrast, over the past decade six women have been elected to the same position. There is no doubt that AMS has grown and evolved. Strong leadership and generous members mean that we now bestow many fellowships, awards, and subventions, most of which did not exist at our last meeting in Philadelphia in 1984. The Society also continues to challenge members to do more, whether by volunteering to help meet our goals, by reaching out to the public, or by improving the experiences of various AMS constituencies. With an eye toward the future, my remarks will address that last task, by focusing on one of our largest and most significant constituencies, our student members. I believe that we all need to be actively involved in finding creative solutions to the major challenges today's students face. As part of this effort, I also encourage all of our student members to make the most of the AMS by seeking greater involvement and ownership in the Society.

Students comprised more than twenty-five percent of our Society last year, accounting for around nine hundred individual memberships. Our rate of student participation is at the high end of the spectrum compared to other scholarly societies in music, art, history, and literature. With these nine hundred students in mind (as well as their many colleagues who have yet to join the AMS), I would like to read a few comments made by a former AMS President:

Celebrating the American Musicological Society at Seventy-five, pp. 33–37. Copyright © 2011 by the American Musicological Society, Inc. All rights reserved. Please direct all requests for permission to photocopy or reproduce article content through the American Musicological Society web site, www.ams-net.org/contact.php.

> There are problems ahead. The job market has been tight in recent years, just at a time when students are completing graduate work in musicology in record numbers, and there are predictions that the situation will not improve in the immediate future. This is a matter of concern for all of us, a matter I think we cannot afford to ignore. . . [Let's] take time to discuss critical matters affecting the professional lives of our members and the future of our discipline.

This message, published in the *AMS Newsletter* by Charles Hamm in January 1973, has a familiar ring—by now AMS audiences have grown accustomed to hearing these sorts of remarks. We are, after all, a society founded during the Great Depression. As AMS President in 1994, Ellen Rosand expressed similar concerns about "the welfare of our student members, many of whom are gradually (and justifiably) becoming disillusioned by the dismal state of the job market."[1] If the scholarly exchanges that have taken place in print and online over the past year are representative of our Society, then such issues remain vivid for many in attendance today. Opinions vary on whether we are experiencing a temporary downturn or have entered into a permanent condition. Whatever the case, last year's job market certainly felt harsh; some observers estimated a total of sixty-five available tenure-track jobs in the fields of musicology and ethnomusicology in 2008–09. Even fewer jobs have been announced this year. Although the present situation may not be unprecedented, it is fair to say that we are in the midst of an employment crisis that affects an enormous percentage of AMS members, and the type of crisis many other members have experienced before.

Unfortunately, these challenges may be with us for the foreseeable future, considering the state of the economy, the shifting nature of higher education, and the decrease in full-time music-related jobs both in and out of academia. It is therefore not surprising to encounter anger or frustration in private conversations and on blogs, web sites, the AMS-list, and various scholarly forums. You may have read the *New York Times* op-ed piece by Melody Rod-Ari, an art history graduate student who, after glimmers of hope, concluded: "Almost finished with my degree, I am faced with the reality that there may be no place for me."[2] I believe the present situation deserves not only our empathy but also a stronger dose of ingenuity from our Society and its individual members.

During the past twenty-five years alone, the AMS has become an extraordinarily well-funded organization that offers extremely generous support to students in the form of fellowships, grants, and other opportunities. But is this enough at this moment? How else might we help students prepare for the future? What do our students need most and how can we work toward achieving these goals? Let me begin to address these questions by outlining my own set of possible strategies to assist and empower our student members. I hope to stimulate discussion and lead in productive directions.

---

1. "President's Message," *AMS Newsletter* 14, no. 2 (August 1994): 2.

2. Melody Rod-Ari, "My 'Irrelevant' Field, the Humanities," *New York Times*, 26 July 2009.

My initial suggestion recalls what took shape in 1973 in response to Charles Hamm's comments. With support of Neal Zaslaw, then chair of the Program Committee, the AMS devoted a full session to issues surrounding the job crisis. Barry Brook led a panel titled "Musicology as a Profession" that dealt with the crisis in higher education and training, jobs, and prospects. I suggest we consider scheduling a similar panel during one of our new daytime program slots in Indianapolis. This could serve as a forum in which we can gauge how present conditions have affected student needs, garner suggestions from AMS members who have faced similar challenges, and learn how our colleagues across the nation are thinking about this issue and acting on it. For this kind of event, I believe it is especially critical to involve student members as panel participants or organizers, in order to gain their input and hear their perspectives.

I also encourage all of our student members to become even more actively engaged with the AMS by seeking further representation within the Society. Some students participate on the AMS council; others are members of selected AMS committees; many more present papers at local or national meetings. But students might emulate their cohorts in other scholarly societies, such as the American Studies Association, the Society for Ethnomusicology, and the Society for American Music, where student committees play an integral role. Such student committees, typically run by six to ten student volunteers, often with input from a faculty advisor, make all kinds of contributions. These may include managing student e-mail lists, circulating information about opportunities for students, recruiting new student members, or bringing student concerns to the attention of the Society's Board of Directors. For annual conferences student committees usually stage student-friendly social events and activities, design panels about topics of particular interest to students, and organize student-only forums. In addition to building community and improving communication within a scholarly society, these groups stay in contact with their colleagues in other organizations to exchange information and collect fresh ideas. Student committees could prove helpful for our Society. There are many types of questions I believe these student groups could help to answer. Would it be productive to hold an open forum at the AMS meeting devoted to student issues? Would students find it useful for AMS to offer additional mentoring assistance, such as putting them in touch with faculty members outside their home institution? What programs or services offered by other scholarly societies would appeal to AMS student members?

Student committees often generate their own events, but they can also work productively in conjunction with other committees. I imagine that an AMS student committee would share common ground with our Committee on Career-Related Issues, an extremely active group that stages conference events about teaching, publishing, grant writing, alternative careers, and more. Together, the two groups might consider organizing a joint session that would tap into the experience of our membership to confront wider institutional challenges. What about a panel that explores how faculty and students can best interface with university administrators? (Let's call it "Managing Your Dean.") Because we are fortunate to have many AMS members who have served as administrators, perhaps we can convince one of them to be a panelist, and learn from his or her experience. The panel could address questions such as:

- What successful approaches have faculty and students used to save or expand music curricula?

- What are useful strategies to preserve faculty lines, create new faculty positions, or convince administrators to fund joint interdisciplinary positions?

- Can AMS as an institution be helpful in this process?

I can imagine similar ties forming between a student committee and our current efforts in the areas of Cultural Diversity as well as Membership and Professional Development. My personal experience suggests that students treasure greater ownership in scholarly societies. Such an AMS student committee could help make all of us more aware of student concerns, and could give one quarter of our membership a greater voice.

Our talented and resourceful student members have taught us much over the years. Their intellectual creativity is of course on display at every conference, because the AMS is noteworthy for providing opportunities for so many students to present their work at our annual meetings—unlike conferences in some of our peer disciplines. We can also look to the long-standing success of student-run journals such as *Current Musicology, repercussions,* and the innovative online journal, *ECHO*. Formed a decade ago, *ECHO* took advantage of the multimedia possibilities offered by web publishing—a novel approach at the time, but one that has since spread to many other music journals. Acknowledging that members of younger generations often are the ones to turn first to new modes of publishing and communication, I wonder whether we are doing enough as a society, or in our roles as individual members in the field, to recognize the value of alternative modes of presentation and publishing, whether as part of graduate admissions, hiring procedures, or tenure dossiers. Today's music students at every level use and value new forms of communication, and I hope that we will seek ways to reward anyone who can reach them effectively by any means. I am thinking in part of the many thoughtful blogs published by AMS members, which you can find linked on our Society's web site. Someday down the road, I would not be surprised if there were an AMS award created to recognize musicological achievement through alternative publishing outlets.

I believe our Society can only profit by reaching out to its members and the general public using even more lines of communication. It is true that we employ a variety of means already: the list-serv, the web site, the newsletter, Bob Judd's email reminders, an RSS feed, and even a twitter feed (yes, an AMS twitter feed is currently spreading the latest AMS news.) But is it possible to do more? Can selected highlights of conferences or forums like this one be made available as podcasts? Is an AMS member dreaming up an irresistible iPhone applet or developing an intensely musicological application with Google Maps? I imagine so. Is there more our Society wishes to do with Facebook or other forms of social networking? What is the latest communication technology emerging just around the bend? I enjoy and appreciate everything we have in place today, but I know that each successive generation of students communicates using different means and with changing expectations. Perhaps some technologically savvy members, whether current or former students, would be interested in contributing ideas or lending a hand.

To underscore how valuable it can be for students to become involved in this society, I would like to conclude my talk by recalling an encounter during my first AMS conference. My goals were simple that year. I wanted to attend papers, to avoid saying anything really embarrassing, and to meet a few scholars whose work I admired (or perhaps just to see them from across a room). I noticed in the program that meetings were scheduled for a Committee on Cultural Diversity, and although I was not exactly sure what that meant, I was interested in learning more. The co-chair of the committee at that time was a professor named Guthrie Ramsey, whose work was familiar to me. What I didn't know is just how tough it would be to corner him. Eventually I found an opportunity, and I asked him about the committee, hoping for a brief, courteous reply. What I got, however, was something very different. Professor Ramsey offered me an extraordinarily gracious invitation to attend the committee's events and to observe its gatherings. Later that year, he invited me to join the committee as a student representative.

That meeting has always shaped how I view AMS—as a place where fruitful encounters can happen and where I could find like-minded colleagues in the midst of all the commotion. The experience of working with the Committee on Cultural Diversity, which seeks to increase the participation of underrepresented groups within AMS and also arranges thematic panels and forums, at first led to making new friends and working alongside prospective mentors. Because of my association with the committee, I have watched promising students attend the AMS conference—with support from the Eileen Southern Travel Fund—then apply and enroll in graduate school, write dissertations, and land jobs. There are dozens of people I look forward to seeing at AMS conferences as a result of these experiences.

I cannot claim that ours was a typical AMS encounter. I recognize that I was fortunate to talk to the right person about the right thing at the right moment. And because I know how many times I have barely managed a quick hello while rushing from one room to another, I would like to try to make up for that a little bit by inviting all student members, as well as all former students to contact me if you have suggestions for how AMS might better serve students. My experience on the Cultural Diversity Committee taught me that there was an identifiable need for student volunteers who could help the Society pursue its goals. And I learned that it is our responsibility as members to seek ways to improve the Society through our participation, volunteer work, service, feedback, and support. By definition, students are the future of this Society, but there is no time like the present to become involved. I hope that enterprising students and everyone else in the Society will work together to discover even more pathways by which we can pursue these goals.

Joseph Kerman and Ellen Rosand

James Haar, Lewis Lockwood, Claire Brook

Judith Tick and Nancy Reich

Glenn Watkins, Edmund Bowles, and Richard Crawford

OPUS Campaign co-chairs Anne Walters Robertson and
D. Kern Holoman play "Happy Birthday"

Richard Taruskin draws the winning raffle ticket (Bob Judd holds the bowl)

AMS Council Student Representatives prepare to sing "Happy Birthday"

Tara Browner and Katherine K. Preston in the Book Exhibit,
AMS Annual Meeting, Philadelphia, 2009

The seventy-fifth-anniversary quilt, held by two of its creators,
Mary Natvig and Honey Meconi

An Anniversary Essay

AMS 75: *The American Musicological Society Celebrates a Birthday*

James Haar

INSPIRATION FOR THE TITLE of this essay comes from AMS 50, the Society's nobly conceived and successfully carried out campaign to celebrate the fiftieth anniversary of its founding.[1] As we now complete the *OPUS* campaign commemorating our seventy-fifth birthday, I wish to thank the current officers, particularly the outgoing and incoming presidents, Charles Atkinson and Jane Bernstein, and directors-at-large of the Society for their kind invitation to write this essay, a commission given either because of—or perhaps in spite of—the fact that I am older than the AMS. And as we look back at AMS 50, we should all unite in wishing every success to the current campaign. I can already see that naming names may be imprudent (though I hope not invidious). I would nevertheless like to offer thanks and congratulations to the *OPUS* campaign's founder Jessie Ann Owens, and to its current co-chairs, Anne Walters Robertson and D. Kern Holoman, with a special note on the extraordinary service of the last-named figure: Kern played an active and important role in AMS 50 and now—scarcely seeming a day older—has shared the running of *OPUS*. Although I considered trying to cover the whole of the period from 1950, where Richard Crawford's admirable essay on the early years of the Society stops,[2] I soon realized that this was too big a task. I will leave to

---

1. I wish to thank Robert Judd for his cooperation in answering my queries, and John Roberts, who made a number of useful suggestions, read my text with sympathetic care, and used a light but skillful hand as its editor. Some readers found the first draft of this essay too personal in tone. Charles Atkinson, who commissioned me to write it, went through the text carefully and sympathetically, toning down this element and removing its more egregious manifestations. I am grateful to him for undertaking such an uncongenial task. This essay, although much altered from its original text, remains a personal statement; I do not presume to speak formally or even informally on behalf of the Society.

2. Richard Crawford, *The American Musicological Society, 1934–1984: An Anniversary Essay* (Philadelphia: American Musicological Society, 1984). The real title of Crawford's work is given on p. 1: "American Musicology Comes of Age: The Founding of the AMS." The entire text of the 1984 booklet is available at <http://www.ams-net.org/resources/Anniversary_Essay.pdf>.

Celebrating the American Musicological Society at Seventy-five, pp. 45–59. Copyright © 2011 by the American Musicological Society, Inc. All rights reserved. Please direct all requests for permission to photocopy or reproduce article content through the American Musicological Society web site, www.ams-net.org/contact.php.

James Haar

others a project of writing a full history of the AMS in the years when it reached its half-century anniversary, 1950–1984. My comments, far short of a history, will range over the whole past of the Society, but with emphasis on more recent periods.

The AMS 50 campaign as I recall it was conducted in a buoyant, "can do" atmosphere, a spirit of fun that unified the membership and gave the Society a high-morale character that has lasted for years and is still with us today (the *OPUS*-related testimony volunteered by a number of members, in every age bracket, is heartening proof of its continuance). I remember campaign speeches that were cheered; I have a clear image of the august Reinhold Brinkmann dressed in an AMS 50 sweatshirt and vociferously hawking its duplicates. I'm sure that none of us who attended it has forgotten the members' talent-show concert (Cleveland, 1986) with its memorable vocal, woodwind, and 'cello solos, not to mention President Margaret Bent's ceremonial benefit raffle drawing—of her own name.

The stated goal of raising money to fund dissertation fellowships for students nearing the end of their doctoral programs was something that all members of the Society could support, and a gratifyingly large number did so in tangible form. By 1986 a single AMS 50 Dissertation Fellowship could be awarded; in the next few years there were two, then three, and in 1990 the original goal of five awards was reached. The number of awards since then has varied, with some being of honorary nature because winning candidates received other sources of funding. In 2000 this fellowship was named for one of its most dedicated early supporters, our beloved long-time Treasurer and first Executive Director, Alvin H. Johnson (1914–2000). This fellowship has been and continues to be (it has been included in the current *OPUS* campaign) an important and highly valued feature of the Society, as well as a good indicator of members' interests, increasingly varied but retaining traditional concerns more than one might think. I hope that as our seventy-fifth anniversary draws to a close some special recognition of the Alvin H. Johnson Dissertation Fellowship can be given.

Support for graduate students about to enter our field is obviously an important AMS activity; and we can hope that the Alvin H. Johnson AMS 50 Fellowship program will not only continue but expand in years to come. Several more recently established fellowship and research-funding awards should be mentioned here. These include the Howard Mayer Brown Fellowship (1995), which funds a year of graduate study by a minority student or a member of a group historically underrepresented in our discipline; and the Eileen Southern Travel Fund (1995), supporting minority students' travel to and attendance at the Annual Meeting to learn about our field and about graduate programs in musicology. Travel prizes and funds that are a part of the *OPUS* campaign and which are named for distinguished members of the Society, include the Eugene K. Wolf Travel Fund for European Research (2004), the Janet Levy Fund (2005) for Independent Scholars, the M. Elizabeth C. Bartlet Fund (2007) for Research in France, and the Harold Powers World Travel Fund (2007). New is the Jan LaRue Fund for Research Travel to Europe (2008). As I read over these names, all of them friends for many years, I am happy to think that they, along with those gracing a number of new, *OPUS*-related prizes for books, articles, and editions, will remain present in the minds of current and future members of our Society.

Another vital and increasingly varied activity of the AMS is our support of scholarly publications. First in chronological order is the Society's *Journal*, known the world over as *JAMS* (Otto Albrecht, for years its Business Manager, once said that his assistants in the Philadelphia office of the Society referred to its other publications as "Jellies"), and internationally recognized since its founding sixty-one years ago as one of the leading scholarly periodicals in our field. At first the *Journal*, like its predecessors, the AMS *Papers* and *Bulletin*, was closely linked to the Society's activities, chapter meetings and especially the Annual Meetings. That this was a concern to members is shown in the Report of the Secretary (Edward N. Waters), where we read the Executive Board's decision that

> "the Editor-in-Chief and the Editorial Board shall be under no obligation to any particular paper beyond that of publishing it by title." Conversely no member who writes a paper is obligated to offer it to the *Journal* if he prefers another publishing medium. Obviously this provision is to leave the Editorial Board free to exercise its critical judgment with respect to contributions from members.[3]

In other words, the Society's new journal aimed at professional independence from the comfortable, even clubby atmosphere of the early years of the AMS.

This independence, which we now value as essential to the *Journal*'s character and quality, could not be reached overnight. The business of the Society continued to appear in the *Journal*'s pages; for example, the program of the Annual Meeting continued to be printed, often appearing after the meeting had taken place, until 1969. As the *Journal* grew in size and reputation, the connection with the recorded activities of its sponsoring society became less inevitable—particularly to the many foreign subscribers.

A solution, not immediate and not cheap, was found, first with the appearance (1971) of the *Newsletter* (or re-appearance; there had been one in the Society's early years—superseded by the *Journal*). Published twice yearly, the *Newsletter* contains not only the program of the Annual Meeting and various reports from officers and committees, but a wide variety of news about AMS members and activities, far more than the *Journal* could ever accommodate. Along with the *Journal* editors beginning with Oliver Strunk in 1948, the *Newsletter* editors starting in 1971 with Claude Palisca (who was at the same time President of the Society!) have deserved

---

[3] *JAMS* 1 (1948): 52.

and continue to earn our thanks for the valuable service they have so consistently performed.

Another category of AMS information that was once published in the *Journal* was a membership list. The growth of the Society soon made this impractical, and only in comparatively recent times (1979) was the problem addressed with the annual publication of the AMS Directory, available in hard copy and online; this contains, in addition to a list of members and subscribers, much valuable information about the Society and its activities, publications included. One long-running series that deserves mention here is *Doctoral Dissertations in Musicology* (*DDM*), begun in 1952 by Helen Hewitt, who produced four editions up to 1965, three of them in part sponsored by the AMS. From 1971 to the mid-1990s Cecil Adkins and Alis Dickinson continued to produce new editions, some with the collaboration of the International Musicological Society. *DDM* goes on, now in an easily accessible online version created by Thomas Mathiesen at the Center for the History of Music Theory and Literature at Indiana University, and maintained at the AMS office.

Early in its history the AMS aspired to publish volumes under its own imprint. As early as 1947 the second volume of Dragan Plamenac's edition of the *Collected Works* of Johannes Ockeghem was published as the Society's Studies and Documents no. 1.[4] The first volume (Leipzig, 1927) was printed in a second edition by the AMS in 1959, as Studies and Documents no. 3. No. 2 is the Dunstable *Complete Works*, published in 1953 as part of Musica Britannica, with a revised edition in 1970.[5] Of a projected series of published dissertations, Joseph Kerman, *The Elizabethan Madrigal: A Comparative Study* (1954) was published, in 1962, later followed by works by Ted Reilly and Edgar Sparks.[6] Two final AMS publications should receive mention here. In 1990 the Society published *Essays in Musicology: A Tribute to Alvin Johnson*, a group of studies contributed (in 1988) by former presidents and officers of the Society and edited by Lewis Lockwood, President, and Edward Roesner, chairman of the Publications Committee; nothing for any of us was a greater labor of love than what we contributed to this volume. The long memory of the AMS showed itself in 1992 with the appearance of volume 3 of Ockeghem's *Collected Works*, edited by Richard Wexler with [the late] Dragan Plamenac.

Thanks to bequests from early members of the AMS, including Manfred Bukofzer, Otto Kinkeldey, Gustave Reese, Dragan Plamenac, and Lloyd Hibberd, the Society formed an endowment fund (1971), which has continued to grow and for which continuing gifts are more than welcome. Publications supported by

---

4. Plamenac's manuscript of this volume was prepared in Germany by 1930 but could not be published until after the Second World War, when he made an English edition for the AMS. A second edition of vol. 2 was published by the AMS in 1966.

5. John Dunstable, *Complete Works*, ed. Manfred F. Bukofzer, Musica Britannica 8 (London: Published for the Royal Musical Association and the American Musicological Society by Stainer and Bell, 1953); 2nd ed., ed. Margaret Bent, Ian Bent and Brian Trowell, 1970.

6. Edward R. Reilly's *Quantz and His Versuch* (1971) is drawn from his dissertation of 1958; Edgar H. Sparks, *The Music of Noel Bauldeweyn* (1972), is based on research in his special field.

AMS grants go back as far as 1965, when *The Commonwealth of Music*, a volume honoring Curt Sachs and edited by Gustave Reese and Rose Brandel, appeared; the same year saw the appearance of the first volume (of ten) of Albert Seay's edition of Arcadelt's *Opera omnia*, done in collaboration with the American Institute of Musicology.

In recent years the Publications Committee has turned its attention away from being itself a publisher and toward contributing funds in aid of members' projects accepted by a wide range of university and commercial presses. Since 1975 over a hundred volumes—mostly books, with some thematic catalogues, editions, and translations—have been helped along the road to publication in various ways, ranging from a lowered purchase price through addition of illustrations, useful appendices, accompanying compact discs, material made available online, and the like. No AMS volunteers work harder and more steadily than the Publications Committee; no group has, as I can testify from personal experience, derived greater satisfaction from service rendered. The range of subject matter in these titles, their methodology and indeed ideology—often embracing our sister disciplines of music theory and ethnomusicology and, a bit less often, fields such as social studies, literary criticism, gender studies and visual-arts criticism—is genuinely impressive, as the chronological listing of titles available on the AMS web site shows.[7]

In 1992 the Society announced a new series: AMS Monographs in Music. The idea was for a periodic number of books, demonstrating openly the breadth of the members' interests, to be published by the Society in collaboration with the University of Nebraska Press. The first number in the series was Graeme Boone's *Patterns in Play: A Model for Text Setting in the Early Songs of Dufay*. When Nebraska ceased publishing the series in 1999, it was taken over by Oxford University Press under a new name, AMS Studies in Music. The first volume, Lawrence Zbikowski's *Conceptualizing Music: Cognitive Structure, Theory, and Analysis*, appeared in 2002. Eight volumes have been published to date; and there are several more in the works (see pp. 123–25 for a complete listing of AMS publications).

From the first the Society has been determinedly internationalist in character, representing the interests of its founders and many of its members. This is true to some extent of other national musicological associations, notably the United Kingdom and Germany; others (Italy, Spain, Russia, most smaller nations) have tended to concentrate on study of their own musical culture.[8] National societies have supported—though not often in a direct way—publication of volumes and series drawing on their musical heritage. The lack of such publications on the part of the AMS was for years deplored, and not only by Americanists; during my own tenure as President (1977–78) I issued an informal, and at the time unanswered, call for a "Musica Americana" series in emulation of our Britannic colleagues.

---

[7]. See "Publications supported by AMS Publication Subventions," <http://www.ams-net.org/Books.php>.

[8]. There are signs that this is at least partially changing in Italy; see the journal *Il Saggiatore musicale*.

The most persistent and best focused demands did of course come from Americanists, chief among them Richard Crawford, himself AMS president in 1983–84. Crawford's frustration over what he perceived as the Society's lack of interest can be seen on the concluding page of his anniversary essay, where he says "AMS members' scholarly interest in the music of their own country had barely progressed beyond the level that Oliver Strunk had found 'disappointing' in 1932."[9] Crawford was of course far from limiting himself to complaints; he was already a distinguished Americanist as teacher and scholar, who was to become for the AMS as he was for the Sonneck Society (renamed the Society for American Music) a central figure in his field, a kind of "Mr. America" whose reports at our Annual Meetings, often accompanied by his waving hefty new volumes of the MUSA series (on this see below), have been heartily applauded.

In 1973 Crawford published an article on the eighteenth-century hymnist William Billings, followed in 1976 by *William Billings of Boston* (with D. P. McKay). He was the guiding spirit (officially the Editorial Consultant) of the four-volume *Complete Works of William Billings* (1977–90), edited by Hans Nathan (vol. 2) and Karl Kroeger (vols. 1, 3, and 4), published by the AMS together with the Colonial Society of Massachusetts. In 1988 the AMS established the series *Music of the United States of America* (MUSA), with Richard Crawford as its first Executive Editor and the University of Michigan its host institution. From 1993 to the present MUSA has issued twenty volumes (published by A-R Editions) containing "classical" and popular music, psalmody and jazz, Victorian choral music, Ives songs, a volume of Amy Beach following one of Irving Berlin, one of Dudley Buck preceding one of Earl "Fatha" Hines, two volumes of transcriptions of Native American music: this is a sampling of the stunning variety of the series, a wonderful spotlight on the "American" in our Society. It is fitting that in 2009 a new prize, the Music in American Culture Award, has joined the happily crowded ranks of the Society's prizes for excellence of work in fields of importance to the organization and its membership.

The Society's early and continuing support of publication by its members has been one of the most visible ways in which it has worked toward its goal of advancing research in the various fields of music as a branch of learning and scholarship. This has a personal dimension as well. We engage in research and publication not just for career advancement or vainglorious ends but for the love of it, sometimes mixed with a bit of competitive spirit. Do we publish too much? I don't think so. Some of us publish more than others, some of us are beginning, or continuing, to hope that we will soon break into print. None of us reads everything that Society members publish, whether or not it is supported by the AMS. Many of us go through periods when we publish nothing or next to it. But when we greet one another at national or chapter meetings most of us go fairly quickly from social gossip to "what are you working on now?"—and expect an answer.

---

9. Crawford, *The American Musicological Society*, 19.

As I have said, this is not the place for a full study of the Society during the thirty-five-year period 1950–1984. What we might try to undertake here is a sketch of the discipline of musicology as represented by the AMS during this period. In its early years the Society was influenced by the ideas and methodology of German scholarship, particularly the work of Guido Adler. The International Congress of 1939 and the war years that followed added other elements to this orientation, but a mix of the old and the (then) new can be seen in the 1950 meeting's inclusion of pedagogic papers such as "Principles of Greek Notation" (J. Murray Barbour), "The Importance of Symbols in the Evolution of Music" (Eric Werner), and especially "Scope, Method and Aims of Systematic Musicology" (Charles Seeger), along with "*Caput Redivivum*: A New Source for Dufay's Missa *Caput*" (Manfred Bukofzer) and "The Original Titles of Bach's Works" (Hans David). General and specific topics shared space, and Renaissance papers occupied as much space as, but not more than, the Bach family. Technology had its place: a plenary session, held jointly with the Music Teachers National Association (MTNA), the Music Library Association (MLA), and the College Music Association, later Society (now CMS) participating, on the subject of "LP Phonograph Records."

The twenty-fifth anniversary meeting (Chicago) of 1959 showed a more modern appearance, with papers on Medieval, Renaissance, Baroque and eighteenth-century topics and a real surprise, George Perle on Berg's *Lulu*. Even more surprising, perhaps—though also reminiscent of the Adlerian past—was a joint session with SEM (Society for Ethnomusicology) on "The Role of Oral Tradition in the History of Music." As we might expect, the Society showed itself mindful of its history: at a dinner Gustave Reese chaired an anniversary observance with talks on "The First Twenty-five Years" by Honorary President Otto Kinkeldey and "The Prospect Before Us" by current President Oliver Strunk.

International Musicological Congress, New York: "Light Vs. Chaos,"
New York Herald-Tribune
(26 September 1939)

Mention of these two meetings brings up the names of other musical societies, with which the AMS met jointly. Some of these societies, such as the venerable Music Teachers National Association (MTNA), founded by Theodore Presser in 1876, and the Music Library Association (MLA), established in 1931, are older than the AMS; they have of course their own agenda and have met with our Society only rarely and for a specific purpose. Others, particularly the College Music Society (CMS), founded in 1958, share many of our educational concerns, if with slightly different foci. AMS and the Society for Ethnomusicology (SEM) began, in the Adlerian period, as twin daughters in the *Musikwissenschaft* family. Ethnomusicological topics appeared in the programs of early national and chapter meetings, and the discipline was slighted only with peril as long as Charles Seeger (1886–1979) was active. The Society for Ethnomusicology was founded in 1955, and the redoubtable Seeger, who had been President of the AMS in 1945–46, served as SEM President in 1960–61. Before 1955 ethnomusicologists, depending on their individual interests, had joined either the AMS or the American Anthropological Association. Their parting from both with the founding of the new society seems to have been amicable. In the AMS itself, ethnomusicologists continue to appear on programs, receive support for publications, and win prizes. AMS and SEM have met together from time to time, notably at the *omnium gatherum* of the Toronto meeting in 2000, and will do so again in 2012.

The other two societies with interests closest to those of the AMS, the Society for American Music (SAM) and the Society for Music Theory (SMT), have had, perhaps unsurprisingly, more complex relationships with their parental institution. In the Society's early years American music was a side interest of a number of members but a central concern to a relative few. As more confirmed Americanists embarked on their scholarly careers, discontent over the perceived place given to American music, referred to above, became more acute, with signs of genuine bad feeling evident. The founding in 1973 of the Sonneck Society, later renamed the Society for American Music, relieved this, but some soreness remained, as could be seen in the first annual meeting of the new Society in 1975, where a group of papers said to have been rejected by the AMS was read with expressed approval. I believe that relationships improved with the establishment of MUSA, and that many SAM members continue to belong to the AMS.

The SMT, founded in 1977, presents a different picture, one of abrupt and decidedly hostile break from the AMS. This I remember well since I was AMS President at the time it happened. I was informed that at the forthcoming meeting (1976) of the Midwest Chapter of the Society in Chicago a group of theorists were going to announce a separation from the AMS and the formation of a new association, the Society for Music Theory. Not sure what to do but feeling I had to do something, I asked for permission to address a plenary session of the Chapter Meeting, and made the trip "east" (I was in Seattle at the time, visiting the University of Washington, from which I made several AMS-related trips). I did speak, trying to emphasize the traditional close ties between historians and theorists in our discipline and imploring the latter to rethink their position. After

I finished (politely but not sympathetically heard), Leonard Meyer made a strong and fervent appeal in support of the bond between music theory and history. It was welcome support from a figure of unimpeachable credit, and I was and remain grateful for it; I miss Leonard Meyer's presence very much. The theorists, or more accurately a small group that had assumed a leadership role, were not persuaded. The split did take place, and the Society for Music Theory was founded. Since that time SMT has flourished, and if I may speak for the AMS, the Society has wished them well. We meet together quite frequently and both profit from the contact. As our Society has broadened in choice of subject and methods of approach, so has the SMT undergone change. I now see no sign of the edginess—needless from the start—of thirty years ago.

No one can predict the future, but it is my belief that the Society is now flexible and responsive enough so that it can accommodate a wide spectrum of special interests, making further splits unnecessary. What has happened in recent years is that new groups have been formed, united by specialization of subject either within the Society's framework or in a close neighborly relationship with it. The first of these is represented by Study Groups affiliated with the AMS, coming together at the Society's Annual Meetings as well as on occasions of their own selection. These include the Cold War and Music Study Group, the Ecocriticism Study Group, the Hispanic Study Group, the LGBTQ (Lesbian, Gay, Bisexual, Transgender, Queer) Study Group, and the Pedagogy Study Group. The second group, different from the first in that meetings are held separate from those of the AMS, includes the Society for Seventeenth-Century Music and the Society for Eighteenth-Century Music, both of whom continue a close relationship with the AMS.

Another area in which the Society has in part moved forward, in part returned to its roots, is performance. The Noah Greenberg Award has proved itself over a thirty-year period to be a valuable part of our activities, especially in the area of performance practice. In its early years the Society's Annual Meetings mixed performance with paper sessions. As meetings grew bigger and papers more numerous concerts were moved entirely to evenings and were a mix of professional and amateur programs. This has worked well, with the Local Arrangements Committee doing a consistently fine job. In recent years a new trend has emerged, with the Performance Committee overseeing a fascinating mix of daytime or early evening recitals, interesting ensembles, lecture-recitals, with a genuinely interesting choice of repertory. The audiences for these are in a way impromptu study groups, very welcome additions to the Society's ever-increasing breadth of response to the multifarious world of musical research.

*   *   *

The "sixties" were when I started my career. I got a degree, found a job, joined the AMS; by 1964 I had read a couple of papers, begun to publish, and was on my way without thinking much about what that way was to be. I had written a rather idiosyncratic dissertation but after finishing it settled into becoming a Renaissance scholar pursuing study of the Italian madrigal, an attractive and roomy field. Aside from the usual qualms—was I "doing enough"?, was my work as good as that of my peers?, was I going to get tenure?—I was poking along fairly contentedly.

It thus came as a real shock to me, as it must have to many of my contemporaries, when at the Washington Annual Meeting in December, 1964, the opening plenary session, entitled *Musicology: Trends and Purposes*, was devoted to two papers: Donald M. McCorkle on "A Place for American Studies in American Musicology" and Joseph Kerman on "A Profile for American Musicology," followed by a long discussion, at times turning into a shouting match, the likes of which I at least had never heard at an AMS gathering. McCorkle's paper was unusual in that American music did not often get so much attention focused on it (see above); it certainly provided material for some discussion. Kerman's address was a real bombshell. His later *Contemplating Music* (1985) may have engendered more lasting critical reaction, some of it bordering on the acrimonious; but the uproar in 1964 was unique. Many people spoke; but among them Edward Lowinsky, who evidently felt that he and his whole generation of expatriate scholars were under personal attack, was especially strong in responding, with a counter-attack—so much so that the whole occasion became known as the "Kerman-Lowinsky Flap." Kerman published his paper in the first number of volume 18 (1965) of *JAMS*; Lowinsky's considered response followed in the next number.[10]

It is not for me to say who won, or even to take sides in this debate; I do encourage readers to look them up and read them with care. To me the dispute is important enough to try to summarize here, as a kind of watershed in the history of our Society. It led to similar arguments on different topics but not unlike it in character, which ruffled the calm musicological sea some twenty years later.

Kerman begins his "Profile" by recognizing a volume dealing with the discipline of musicology in a general way, written by Frank Harrison, Mantle Hood, and Claude Palisca, and published in 1963.[11] He starts by saying that Palisca considers the musicologist to be "first and foremost" a historian, that Harrison thinks the scholar should be more of a "sociologist," by which we would probably mean a cultural historian, and that the ethnomusicologist Hood more or less agrees with Harrison. The more thoughtful music historians try to write cultural history, he says, thinking perhaps of Curt Sachs and especially of Paul Henry Lang.[12] The less thoughtful ones collect a lot of information "in the vague expectation that someone—someone else—will find it useful" (p. 62). Kerman was speaking soon after the appearance of several large "period" volumes, all of them issued by the

---

10. Joseph Kerman, "A Profile for American Musicology," *JAMS* 18 (1965): 61–69; Edward E. Lowinsky, "Character and Purposes of American Musicology: A Reply to Joseph Kerman," *JAMS* 18 (1965): 222–34.

11. Frank Ll. Harrison, Mantle Hood, and Claude V. Palisca, *Musicology,* Humanistic Scholarship in America: The Princeton Studies, ed. Richard Schlatter (Englewood Cliffs, NJ: Prentice-Hall, 1963).

12. Curt Sachs, *The Rise of Music in the Ancient World, East and West* (New York: W. W. Norton, 1943); Paul Henry Lang, *Music in Western Civilization* (New York: W. W. Norton, 1941).

Norton press.[13] Was he attacking them, or rather, as I believe, smaller studies and papers consisting largely of factual information, sometimes very dull when read aloud? In any event, he uses rather strong language.

What Kerman champions is criticism, which he views as the highest stage of musical scholarship, indeed one to which all other historical research and analytic theory are preparatory steps. Criticism is, at its best, an aesthetic field that can seriously inform all of us, inside and outside the normally defined field of musical studies, about human values in great works of musical art. These latter are for Kerman what students should be working on, not some unnamed *Kleinmeister* or obscure repertory (he does not say whether the musicologists whom he finds so dull would somehow be transformed into perceptive and articulate critics if they do so).

If this were to happen, American musicology would turn away from the German tradition which, carried on faithfully in American colleges and universities, has stood in the way of the development of a truly American musicology; it is time for new leadership to strike out new paths. The AMS has grown in size (to 1,800 members, he says) but is still in its infancy, compared to fields like art history and English. Only—apparently—through a turn to genuinely humanistic criticism can it grow to maturity.

That a speech like this would raise hackles can come as no surprise. Edward Lowinsky responded sharply to it as member of a panel in the lively discussion period. He doubtless knew that Kerman was planning to publish his speech in a forthcoming issue of *JAMS*, and so arranged to have an expanded version of his response appear in the following one.[14] Dividing his response into three sections, Lowinsky begins by coming to the defense of what Kerman regards as preparatory steps such as transcriptions and editions (mainly of pre-1600 music, though Kerman does not say so), archival work (also mainly concerned with old music), bibliography, etc. These all represent to Lowinsky special skills, worth pursuing for their own sake as well as, or even without, the "summit" of criticism. Lowinsky goes on to say something really prophetic about music criticism, namely that it does not stand at the top of a pyramid of other kinds of musicological research but that

> it must develop an entirely new set of questions, and along with them new methods and criteria of answering them. In the task of developing the right kind of questions and criteria, musical criticism is much closer to criticism in literature or the visual arts than it is to a whole number of musical sciences.[15]

---

13. Gustave Reese, *Music in the Middle Ages* (1950); idem, *Music in the Renaissance* (1954; rev. ed. 1959); Manfred F. Bukofzer, *Music in the Baroque Era, from Monteverdi to Bach* (1947); Alfred Einstein, *Music in the Romantic Era* (1947).

14. See above, n. 10. Kerman wrote a counter-response, appearing as a Communication in *JAMS* 18 (1965): 426–27.

15. "Character and Purposes of American Musicology," 224.

One should remember that this was written in a period when New Criticism was still *au courant*, affecting a number of fields as well as literature—though not, as yet, musicology.

In the second part of his response Lowinsky criticizes Kerman's idea that the critic stands alone and above others as a kind of "lord of the manor." In answer Lowinsky piles up examples of American and international musicological achievements of the past twenty years. Not all of these are completely relevant to his argument, though his citation of Alfred Einstein's *The Italian Madrigal* is unanswerably appropriate.[16] It is in the third section of his paper that the temperature, high to start with, rises close to feverish. Lowinsky attacks Kerman's view of musicology as a discipline with a strong national character everywhere but in the U.S., where it remains subservient to the German tradition. Kerman had urged American musicologists to separate themselves "from an older alien tradition" ("Profile," 67) and to find leadership in a native generation younger than that of German and German-trained scholars. Another scholar might have shrugged this off; Lowinsky clearly took it personally. Rather than defend himself and his fellow expatriate scholars he refers darkly to Kerman's use of "alien" and "native" as hinting at Nazi and Communist attitudes toward scholarship. Lowinsky finishes his piece with a more positive note, an encomium to the peculiarly American nature of the "young generation" of musicologists (what we might term the Grout-Palisca generation).

The Kerman-Lowinsky clash changed the Society's view of itself, beginning a process of self-examination that by degrees brought us from basically contented "infancy" (as Kerman would have it) through an intermittently stormy "adolescence" in the eighties and nineties to what in the decade just ending I shall cautiously but optimistically call a "young-adult" stage. By this I mean that beginning in the 1970s but gathering momentum in the next two decades musicologists, especially younger ones entering the profession after growing up in the era of Vietnam-war turbulence, were intellectually restless, looking for new subject matter, new methodologies, even new ideologies. As they did this they began to reach outside the boundaries of their own discipline as well as beyond the limits of the Western European musical tradition.

The fields indicated as promising by Kerman, English literature and art history, were of course natural places to turn, but concentrated study of single works of art were not all there was to look at. Ideological currents of a broader nature were affecting these fields and others, such as history—indeed almost all areas except for the natural sciences. One of these, gender studies, was rather slow to start in musicology, but was to become one of the most important new fields within the AMS.

Yet another area of study to gain currency in the seventies was that of popular music. Paralleling the rise of African-American studies and interwoven with them to some extent, popular music was not part of music curricula or the subject of many scholarly papers in the early years of the decade. The extent to which it was

---

16. Alfred Einstein, *The Italian Madrigal*, trans. A. H. Krappe, Roger Sessions, and Oliver Strunk (Princeton: Princeton University Press, 1949).

to grow in both respects has pleased some of us and surprised almost all of us, but it should have been predictable. I well remember listening to the complaints and "non-negotiable demands" of undergraduate rebels in the late sixties and early seventies, wanting to know why "we" did not include "their" music, by which they meant post-Beatles pop and rock repertory, in the curriculum. Some of these undergraduates (at New York University, in my case) went on to graduate school and became musicologists; they and their students are now "we." It should thus not be too surprising that popular music has become an important element in the increasingly mixed palette of musicological study and writing.

When I think of the current scene, what I have called our "young-adult" phase, I perceive not a backward swing of the pendulum but a gently resistant push of traditional (sometimes with reformist tendencies) musicology, including early-music studies, toward better representation at our meetings and in at least a few of our educational institutions. For a time the enemies of the so-called New Musicology were not so much positivist historians as they were hard-core theorists who held nothing—including popular song—immune from analytical scrutiny. A softening of edges is now evident among both historians and theorists, resulting in at least some betterment of relations.

I do not feel competent, or unbiased, enough to speak in any detail about the various new directions the Society and its members have embarked upon, most markedly in the last twenty-five years. Joseph Kerman has of course repeated and updated his views during this time, notably in *Contemplating Music* (1985). This book has been widely discussed, notably in a spirited rebuttal by Margaret Bent and a qualifiedly favorable review-essay, magisterial in tone, by Leo Treitler.[17] Rather than *Contemplating Music*, though, I should like to turn to another of Kerman's works, his article "American Musicology in the 1990s," as a lens through which to view some of the most recent developments in the field.[18]

Restricting himself to historical musicology, Kerman begins by talking about "fruitful grafts" from areas outside music, specifying structuralist and poststructuralist theory, anthropology, feminism, and "ideology critique"; he later singles out individual scholars who have made or are making moves into such areas. In general, he says

> Musicologists have addressed themselves on various levels to problems of interpretation or hermeneutics. They have probed the relations between music, society, and politics in deeper ways than before. They have begun to investigate issues of gender and sexual orientation in music. Ricoeur, Adorno, Gadamer, Geertz, de Man, Cixous, and other pan-intellectuals have been making an appearance in

---

17. Margaret Bent, "Fact and Value in Contemporary Musical Scholarship," the opening piece in a panel of the same name, published by the College Music Society (Boulder, CO) in 1986; Leo Treitler, review (subtitled "The Power of Positive Thinking") in *JAMS* 42 (1989): 375–402.

18. Joseph Kerman, "American Musicology in the 1990s," *Journal of Musicology* 9 (1991): 131–44. See also Kerman's essay in *Tendenze e metodi nella ricerca musicologica: Atti del convegno internazionale (Latina 27–29 settembre 1990)*, ed. Raffaele Pozzi (Florence: Olschki, 1995): 11–27.

footnotes; and often enough their thought has surged up from the footnotes to activate the musicological text itself.[19]

Adding names such as Lacan and Derrida to the list, musicologists heard the call, and what were initial probings and investigations in the eighties became more and more common in the nineties. In the present decade at least some, such as gender-sexuality studies, have established orthodoxies in much the same way as traditional orthodoxies had crystallized a couple of generations ago.

Looking specifically at publications in book form, Kerman singles out anthologies based on new musicological approaches, of which he names six published or begun in the late eighties.[20] Of these I think the most influential are the Leppert-McClary *Music and Society*, partly for its message that musical art of every kind and at every level is highly politicized and that musical scholarship must follow, and partly from the near-brutalist vehemence of its language; and the Solie volume, *Musicology and Difference*, on feminist concerns, including sexual preference. Fifteen, perhaps even ten years ago, *Authenticity and Early Music* might have been of equal importance as affecting musicologists of every stripe. Since that time performance of early music has of course continued, but the question of "authenticity," whether or not resolved in favor of a negative view (as unattainable or even a chimera), has curiously receded, at least in my experience, from the scene almost completely. Being new, it would seem, is no guarantee of long prominence. To conclude his essay Kerman names some newly published books he can recommend, and singles out four scholars as distinguished practitioners of new directions in musicology; they serve, in his words, to "go some way toward fleshing out the dry statistics which were presented earlier" (p. 141).

At least two presidents of the Society have to my knowledge spoken about the New Musicology—to employ an unhappy but commonly used (these days perhaps a bit less commonly) umbrella term—at Annual Meetings. Lewis Lockwood in 1987 (New Orleans) warned of "ephemeral and subjective verbal formulations to describe musical context" and of a danger in teaching or advocating new critical and ideological theories "to beginners and students who may lack all substantial and traditional musical experience and have little or no idea of the theoretical

---

19. "American Musicology in the 1990s," 132. Much of what follows refers to Kerman's article. Of interest, but there is no space for it here, is *Musicology in the 1980s: Methods, Goals, Opportunities*, ed. D. Kern Holoman and Claude V. Palisca (New York: Da Capo, 1982).

20. These are 1) *Music and Society: The Politics of Composition, Performance, and Reception*, ed. Richard Leppert and Susan McClary (Cambridge: Cambridge University Press, 1987); 2) *Authenticity and Early Music: A Symposium*, ed. Nicholas Kenyon (Oxford: Oxford University Press, 1988); 3) *Reading Opera*, ed. Arthur Groos and Roger Parker (Princeton: Princeton University Press, 1988); 4) *Music and Text: Critical Enquiries*, ed. Steven Scher (Cambridge: Cambridge University Press, 1992); 5) *Disciplining Music: Musicology and Its Canons*, ed. Philip V. Bohlman and Katherine Bergeron (Chicago: University of Chicago Press, 1992); 6) *Musicology and Difference: Gender and Sexuality in Music Scholarship*, ed. Ruth A. Solie (Berkeley: University of California Press, 1993).

and systematic bases of musical thought."[21] Ellen Rosand's "The Musicology of the Present," an address delivered in 1994 (Minneapolis), has a good deal to say about the New Musicology, most of it favorable and expressed in a welcoming tone. Her warning is against exclusionary approaches, even attacks on traditional musicological work, made by over-committed or over-enthusiastic partisans of some recently introduced idea.[22]

Of course we have all been, and will continue to be, affected by new ideologies, new methodologies, new ways of writing or even listening to papers. We have all, young and old, been changed in greater and smaller ways, through reading or listening or a kind of scholarly osmosis by the advent of so many new ideas and approaches in the study of our beloved discipline. For some of us the subject itself has been altered almost beyond recognition;[23] but I hope that most of us accept, or will come to accept, even to admire the very mix of old and new interests and approaches that now characterize the scholarly study of music in the broadest sense. This is my birthday toast to the American Musicological Society on its seventy-fifth anniversary.

---

21. Cited by Treitler, review of Kerman, *Contemplating Music*, 377, 402. The complete text of Lockwood's Presidential Address is in *College Music Symposium* 28 (1988), 1–9.

22. Rosand's address is printed in the AMS *Newsletter* 25, no. 1 (February 1995): 10–11, 15.

23. A view advanced (but not originated) by a colleague is that the Great Change in our discipline came with the abandonment of the deckle-edge cover of *JAMS*, which took place in vol. 50, no. 1 (Spring, 1997).

Treasurer James Ladewig and President Jane A. Bernstein

Elaine Sisman, J. Peter Burkholder, and H. Colin Slim

H. Colin Slim, Anne Walters Robertson,
and Jessie Ann Owens

Isabelle Cazeaux

Hans Tischler

Maynard Solomon and Robert Marshall

Charles M. Atkinson and Lawrence F. Bernstein

Howard Smither, James Pruett, Edmund Bowles, Bruno Nettl, and Lillian Pruett

Leo Treitler, Wye Jamison Allanbrook, and Margaret Bent

Documents from the AMS Archives

Documents from the AMS Archives 67

Otto Kinkeldey
President, 1935–36 and 1941–42

Manfred Bukofzer
Board member, five terms from
1942 to 1955

Gustave Reese
President, 1951–52

Alvin H. Johnson
Treasurer, 1970–93;
Executive Director, 1983–93

Alfred Einstein
Vice President, 1945–46

Eileen Southern
Board member, 1974–75

Otto E. Albrecht
Treasurer, 1954–70

Janet Knapp
President, 1975–76

Documents from the AMS Archives   69

Paul Henry Lang
Treasurer, 1936–50

Oliver Strunk
President, 1959–60

George S. Dickinson
President, 1947–48

Donald J. Grout
President, 1953–54 and 1961–62

AMERICAN MUSICOLOGICAL SOCIETY

3 East 43rd Street,
New York, N.Y.,
November 14, 1934.

On June 3, 1934, a meeting was held in New York by a group consisting of Miss Helen H. Roberts and Messrs. George Dickinson, Carl Engel, Joseph Schillinger, Charles Louis Seeger, Harold Spivacke, W. Oliver Strunk, Joseph Yasser, and Gustave Reese. The group declared itself an organization, to which the name AMERICAN MUSICOLOGICAL SOCIETY has since been given. At the meeting, Dr. Otto Kinkeldey was elected President and an Organizing Committee was appointed. Dr. Kinkeldey has accepted office. The Organizing Committee has drafted a Constitution and a set of By-Laws, copies of which are enclosed herewith.

You are cordially invited to become a Member of the Society.

On December 1 next, at 4 P.M., a general meeting will be held in the Rehearsal Room at the club-house of the Beethoven Association, 30 West 56th Street, New York, N.Y. to adopt the Constitution and By-Laws, to elect officers other than the President, and to transact such other business as may come up. I hope you will be able to attend for the purpose of joining the organization and voting. If you should be unavoidably prevented from attending, I should appreciate your sending me a letter signifying your willingness to become a Member.

Very sincerely yours,

GR:RS   Secretary of the Organizing Committee.

Gustave Reese, letter of invitation to become a member of the newly-founded American Musicological Society (14 November 1934)

Documents from the AMS Archives

Approved membership application slips for Alfred Einstein and Arnold Schoenberg (1939)

Mr. Joseph Yasser - #2   December 9, 1935

Department of Hunter College.

I have received an application for membership from Mr. Donald J. Grout, Mills College, California. I, therefore, nominate him under the By-Law to Article III B I. He recently returned from two years of study in Europe, on a Harvard Fellowship.

I have received an application for membership from Miss Rosalie Housman, 115 East 90 Street, New York, N. Y., and therefore nominate her under the By-Law to Article III B I. I should add, however, that Miss Housman is not a person I should nominate if the By-Laws did not require me to do so. She attended a meeting of the Greater New York Chapter on November 3, as a guest, and embroidered throughout the meeting (!) I do not believe her personality fits her for membership. It is only fair to add, however, that she made her application at what she says was the suggestion of Dr. Leichtentritt. She is a fairly active composer and is (or was) the New York representative of the Pacific Coast Musician.

I have received an application for membership from Mr. Edwin Hughes, 338 West 89 Street, New York, N. Y., and therefore nominate him under the By-Law to Article III B I. Mr. Hughes is, I believe, too well known for a thumb-nail sketch of him to be necessary.

I have received an application for membership from Mrs. Margaret McNamara Mott, Grosvenor Library, Buffalo, New York. I, therefore, nominate her under the By-Law to Article III B I. Mrs. Mott is Music Librarian of the Grosvenor Library.

May I ask you to add any further information concerning the nominees that you may wish forwarded to the Executive Board, and may I also ask you to make your recommendations.

                                        Sincerely yours,

                                        Gustave Reese
GR:AM   Secretary

O.K. except Miss R. Housman

Letter from Gustave Reese to Joseph Yasser nominating Donald J. Grout, Edwin Hughes, and Margaret McNamara Mott, but not Rosalie Housman, to membership (9 December 1935)

Documents from the AMS Archives

[page 1, top fragment:]

not have admitted Beethoven, Wagner, Brahms, ~~Wagner~~, Schönberg etc. in case they had desired to be our members. I am speaking here only for myself, and the committee on admission can of course refuse to accept Miss Housman. But as you asked for my opinion, I give it here quite frankly.

Very sincerely Yours
H. Leichtentritt

[page 2:]

993 Memorial Drive.
Cambridge. Mass.
Jan. 27. 1936.

American Musicological Society.

Dear Mr. Ries:

I have received the list of new members proposed. I have no objections to raise, and would like to see all 18 candidates for admission received as members. Regarding No. 17, Miss Rosalie Housman, I am not of the opinion of the ~~com~~ Membership committee, who propose to reject her application. As I know Miss Housman since many years — she has been my pupil in Berlin twice — I am convinced of her fitness and ability to be a member. She is just now giving a course of lectures in N.Y. which is well received, and she is quite well versed in history of music, theory, etc. To reject her, because she was seen embroidering during a meeting seems to me a little ridiculous. Granted, that I myself do not like such a breach of correct behaviour and social etiquette: but is our society concerned with the more or less elegant manners of our members? Most of us musicians are queer fellows in some way or other and we often sin as regards correct manners. After such a precedent I am afraid quite a number of us will have to be thrown out sooner or later for some reason akin to embroidering, or disturbing in some way sensitive members. We could on such grounds

Letter from Hugo Leichtentritt to Gustave Reese regarding Rosalie Housman (27 January 1936)

Report of the Publication Committee of the American Musicological Association

It is proposed that the Association have a publication of its own to be known as the Bulletin of the American Musicological Association, said Bulletin to consist in the beginning of not more than 16 pages (without a stock cover), and to be published in quantities of 1000, two or more times a year. Sample mast-heads, in proof, are submitted herewith. It is estimated by G. Schirmer that 1,000 copies of such a Bulletin would cost the Association $110.00 per issue to manufacture. It is estimated that the cost of mailing 1,000 copies of the bulletin would be $30.00 per issue. The total estimated cost of manufacturing and mailing would be $140.00 per issue.

Since the Bulletin would necessarily be limited to brief articles, news, reviews, etc., The Musical Quarterly would open its pages to longer papers by members of the Association. The Quarterly would pay for these at its usual rates. It would assign 100 pages a year, or not more than two articles per issue, to papers submitted through the Publication Committee of the Association, the final selection of papers to be published to be subject to the approval of the Editor of The Musical Quarterly. In the captions of such articles there could be a notation, under the name of the contributor, designating him as a member of the Association.

August 29, 1934.

First report of the Society's Publication Committee, outlining their proposals for the *Bulletin* and an assigned section of *The Musical Quarterly* (29 August 1934)

Columbia University
in the City of New York
DEPARTMENT OF MUSIC

July 14, 1936.

Dear Reese:

    I received the Bulletin with great pleasure. It is a most creditable job and ought to make people realize that this is a serious organization. I am especially pleased at the prospect of causing an agreeable surprise in Europe.
    I wonder whether institutions such as the Columbia Library cannot obtain a copy of the Bulletin? We should like to have them on file. Perhaps we can admit institutions for membership. The French Society does, or perhaps we can sell the Bulletin for 25 cents a piece. May I also offer a suggestion? I think it would look better if you could mail them in a larger envelope so that they won't be folded.
    I aknowledge with thanks the check you sent me for my article and the six copies of the issue of the Quarterly. I do not think that I will notify people in the " high powered " manner you suggested in your letter, but I should like to distribute a few copies. How about some separate prints? I usually get some, at a nominal price, from other periodicals.
    How is your magnum opus coming along? By this time you should be putting on the finishing touches.
    Everything is quiet around here and I am working like a Republican campaigner. Let me know if you are in town perhaps we can swelter together some evening.

    Cordially

    P. H. L.

Letter from Paul Henry Lang to Gustave Reese regarding the publication of the Society's first *Bulletin* (14 July 1936)

PROGRAM

International Congress of the American Musicological Society

Held in
NEW YORK, N. Y.

SEPTEMBER 11-16, 1939

MONDAY, SEPTEMBER 11th

BEETHOVEN ASSOCIATION CLUB-ROOMS, 30 WEST 56TH STREET, CONGRESS HEADQUARTERS

Founded in 1918 by Harold Bauer, this organization has as its object the bringing together of artists of established reputation to give concerts in a spirit of artistic fraternity. None of the member-artists receives any remuneration, and the net proceeds are donated for purposes of general musical interest determined by vote of the members.

9:30 Registration; Welcome to North and South American and European guests

11:00 Concert of American Chamber Music by the ROTH STRING QUARTET: J. K. Paine, Op. 5; Arthur Foote, *Night Piece;* Quincy Porter, Quartet No. 4; Roy Harris, Three Preludes and Fugues

12:45 Luncheon. Speech by the President of the American Musicological Society. Entertainment: Alan Lomax singing ballads to his guitar. Keynote of the Congress (Reservations must be made in advance with Assistant Secretary Angell or Chase)

2:30 Annual Business Meeting of the American Musicological Society
(*Open to members only*)

WORLD'S FAIR GROUNDS, FLUSHING
(*Take Subway from Fifth Avenue & 53rd Street; admission to Fair Grounds, 75 cents*)

5:15 Visit Fine Arts Building (*admission, 40 cents*). Make tour of grounds

7:00 Supper at Brazilian Pavilion (Reservations must be made in advance with Assistant Secretary Angell or Chase)
Welcome by Grover Whalen

9:30 Fire-Fountain Display

10:30 BILLY ROSE'S AQUACADE or THE HOT MIKADO
(*admission to either, 40 cents to 99 cents*)

International Musicological Congress, New York: program of the meeting (September 1939)

TUESDAY, SEPTEMBER 12th

BEETHOVEN ASSOCIATION CLUB-ROOMS,
30 WEST 56TH STREET

9:30 Opening General Session—
Carleton Sprague Smith, presiding
Charles Seeger (Federal Music Project, Washington, D. C.)—Government and Music: A Field for Applied Musicology
Dragan Plamenac (Yugoslavia)—16th- and 17th-Century Music in Dalmatia (Illustrations by The Madrigalists)
Edward J. Dent (England)—Cavalieri's *Rappresentazione di Anima e di Corpo*
Knud Jeppesen (Denmark)—Venetian Folk-songs of the Renaissance (Illustration by The Madrigalists)
Curt Sachs (New York University—The So-Called Babylonian Notation
Otto Gombosi (Hungary)—New Light on Ancient Greek Music
(*Discussion at discretion of Chairman*)

ROCKEFELLER CENTER, 50TH STREET & 5TH AVENUE

Begun in 1931, this group of 14 buildings covers 12 acres of ground (3 city blocks), replacing 234 buildings and increasing the population of the district from 4,000 to 25,000 permanent residents. To the 2 miles of shops and 70 floors of offices come more than 100,000 visitors a day. Eleven foreign consulates are housed in these buildings, including those of Great Britain, Argentina and Chile.

1:00 Luncheon in the Rainbow Room Lounge (At No. 30 Rockefeller Plaza: Completed in 1932; rises 850 feet in the air) (Reservations must be made in advance with Assistant Secretary Angell or Chase; capacity limited to 100)

2:45 Visit to Radio City; Demonstration of Electronic Orchestra. Welcome by official of National Broadcasting Corporation

NEW YORK PUBLIC LIBRARY,
FIFTH AVENUE & 42ND STREET

Formed in 1895 by the consolidation of The Lenox, Astor, and Tilden Libraries. The New York Public Library, second in the country with more than 3½ million volumes, now stands on the site of the former Croton reservoir, on lands granted to the city in 1686. The building, stretching two city blocks—390 feet long and 270 feet deep—was completed in 1911 from plans by Architects Carrère & Hastings.

5:00 Reception in the Lenox Gallery, followed by Short Instrumental Illustrations of Library Publications, conducted by Sydney Beck

FRAUNCES' TAVERN, 54 PEARL STREET
(*Take East Side I. R. T. Subway from Grand Central to Bowling Green; walk 1 block east and 1 block south*)

Bowling Green—New York's oldest existing Park; originally the open space before the Fort; "the Square" before the house of Burgomaster Martin Cregier, 1660; "The Parade" 1730; leased as a "Bowling Green", 1733; Statue of George III erected 1770, pulled down, 1776.
Fraunces Tavern—Oldest existing structure on Manhattan Island; built as a residence by Etienne De Lancey, 1719; Tavern of Samuel Fraunces (later Steward of Washington's household) and others. Scene of Washington's farewell to his officers, Dec. 4, 1783. Contains a Museum of Revolutionary relics, historic paintings and portraits, etc.

7:00 Supper (Reservations must be made in advance with Assistant Secretary Angell or Chase; capacity limited to 150)

8:30 Concert of THE OLD HARP SINGERS of Nashville, Tennessee; George Pullen Jackson, Founder. Puritan Psalmody; Wesley's Hymns, Charleston, S. C., 1737; Billings' Fuguing Tunes; White Spirituals and Folk Songs

WEDNESDAY, SEPTEMBER 13th

BEETHOVEN ASSOCIATION CLUB-ROOMS,
30 WEST 56TH STREET

9:30 Session on PRIMITIVE AND FOLK MUSIC IN NORTH AMERICA—George Herzog (Columbia University), presiding
George Pullen Jackson (Vanderbilt University)—Art Music *versus* Folk Music
Helen H. Roberts (Tryon, North Carolina)—North American Indian Music
Annabel Morris Buchanan (University of Richmond)—Modal and Other Melodic Aspects of North American Folk Music
Roy Lamson, Jr. (Williams College)—The English Broadside Ballad of the 16th and 17th Centuries and its Tunes

1939 Musicological Congress, New York: Program *(cont.)*

Samuel P. Bayard (Harvard University)—British Folk Music in North America
George Herzog—African Influence in North American Indian Music
(*Discussion at discretion of chairman*)

2:30 Demonstrations of American Indian and Folk Music: Indian Melodies and Dances; Dulcimer player; Old-time fiddler; Folk Music of the White Man (Ballads, Shanteys, Lumberjack Songs); Negro Contributions
Alan Lomax (Washington, D. C.)—Report on the Archives of American Folk Song in the Library of Congress

7:00 Supper (Reservations must be made in advance with Assistant Secretary Angell or Chase)

AUDITORIUM OF THE NEW YORK HISTORICAL SOCIETY
170 Central Park West (Between 76th and 77th Streets)
(Take Independent Subway to 81st Street)
The Society contains American portraits, folk art exhibits, etc.

8:30 Concert of 19th- and 20th-Century American Music by JOHN KIRKPATRICK and assisting artists: Works by Louis Moreau Gottschalk, Edward MacDowell, Roger Sessions, Charles Ives

THURSDAY, SEPTEMBER 14th

HARKNESS AUDITORIUM, COLUMBIA UNIVERSITY LIBRARY BUILDING
(Take West Side I. R. T. Subway to 116th Street and Broadway)
Chartered in 1754 as King's College by George II. The eight students of the class of '54 met in the vestry room of "The New School adjoining Trinity Church on Lower Broadway". In 1760 the college erected its own buildings and twenty-four years later, during the Revolution, it patriotically changed its name to Columbia. In 1857 the college moved to what was then far up town—Madison Avenue and 50th Street—and again in 1897 to its present site.

9:30 Session on MEDIAEVAL AND RENAISSANCE MUSIC—Gustave Reese, presiding
Oliver Strunk (Princeton University)—Certain Aspects of 16th Century Counterpoint

Yvonne Rokseth (France)—Music of the German *Passionsspiele* in the Middle Ages
Albert Smijers (Holland)—Music of the Illustre Lieve Vrouwe Broederschaps in Herzogenbusch 1330-1600
Fernando Liuzzi (Italy)—Notes sur les "Barzelette" et "Canzoni a ballo" italiennes du XVme siècle, d'après des documents inédits
Leonard Ellinwood (East Lansing, Michigan)—The French Renaissance of the 12th Century in Music
Johannes Wolf (Germany)—The Lewis van Gruythuyse Song Collection of the 14th Century
(*Discussion at discretion of the chairman*)

COLUMBIA UNIVERSITY FACULTY CLUB, 400 WEST 117TH STREET
(Walk from Library)

1:00 Luncheon, Paul Henry Láng presiding (Reservations must be made in advance with Assistant Secretary Angell or Chase; see note on last page)

2:00 Visit the University

THE CLOISTERS, FORT TRYON PARK AT 198TH STREET
(Take Independent Subway to 190th Street and walk to the Museum or take the No. 4 Bus up Riverside Drive)
George Gray Barnard, the sculptor, in 1914 opened to the public his fine collection of mediaeval sculpture and architectural material. In 1926 this was augmented by Mr. and Mrs. John D. Rockefeller, Jr., through whose generosity the present building, housing the collection (still further enlarged), was constructed and opened in May, 1938. The plan of the building was developed around the architectural elements comprising much of the collection—large sections of the cloisters of 12th-15th century French monasteries, etc. (Mediaeval musical instruments are represented in the capitals of a few of the cloisterpillars). The collection's 15th-century French Flemish tapestries depicting the Hunting of the Unicorn are the outstanding set of Gothic tapestries in this country.

4:00 Concert of Mediaeval Music by YVES TINAYRE, a Select Choir of the PIUS X SCHOOL OF LITURGICAL MUSIC, and assisting artists: Introit—Requiem aeternam (Gregorian); Kyrie: Alme Pater (Gregorian); Sanctus from Mass III (Gregorian); Responsary—

1939 Musicological Congress, New York: Program *(cont.)*

Canite (Ambrosian); Communion—Passer invenit (Gregorian); Rorate caeli (Gregorian); Offertory—Jubilate Deo universa terra (Gregorian); Haec dies (Léonin); Deum time! (Léonin); Beata viscera (Pérotin); Agniaus douz (13th century); Flos de virga nascitur (13th century); Five Anonymous 13th-century Trouvère Songs; Rose lys printemps (Machaut); Ploures, dames! (Machaut); Adieu, mon amoureuse joye (Binchois); Mille bonjours (Dufay); Vergine bella (Dufay); Alleluia: Angelus Domini (11th-century organum); O miranda-Salve mater-Kyrie (13th-century motet); Puellare gremium (14th-century motet); Qui cum Patre, from the Credo of the Missa Salve diva Parens (Obrecht); Urbs beata Jerusalem (Kunsperger); Flos florum (Dufay)

CLAREMONT INN, RIVERSIDE DRIVE & 124TH STREET

(*Take Bus No. 4 down Riverside Drive*)

The Claremont Inn, once a private house, was built in 1806 by Michael Hogan, an Irish immigrant from County Clare. But the house is said not to have been named for Hogan's County Clare, but after "Claremont", the Royal estate of Prince William [William IV] of England, who had sailed with Hogan as a midshipman in the British navy, later visiting him in America. The house was occupied for a time by the Earl of Devon and in 1815 by Joseph Bonaparte, the ex-King of Spain. The trial trip of the first steamboat, Fulton's *Clermont*, took place opposite this point.

7:00 Supper (Reservations must be made in advance with Assistant Secretary Angell or Chase)

AUDITORIUM OF THE JUILLIARD GRADUATE SCHOOL, 130 CLAREMONT AVENUE (122ND STREET)

(*Walk from Claremont Inn*)

The Graduate School became active in 1924. A year later it merged with the Institute of Musical Art, founded in 1905 by Dr. Frank Damrosch through the benefactions of James Loeb.

8:30 Concert of Unpublished Music by Georg Friedrich Händel, under the direction of J. M. Coopersmith. Soloists: Florence Vickland, soprano; Viola Silva, contralto; Ernst Victor Wolff, harpsichordist; assisted by a chamber orchestra. Diana Cacciatrice (Cantata con stromenti); E troppo bella (Aria); Sarei troppo felice (Cantata a voce sola); Sonata in G minor (Violino, Violoncello obligato e Basso continuo); Handel non può mia Musa (Cantata a voce sola); Sonata in G minor (Due Flauti Traversieri e Basso continuo); Benchè mi sia crudele, from "Ottone" (Aria); Ero e Leandro (Cantata con stromenti); Gli dirai, from "Alessandro Severo" (Duetto)

FRIDAY, SEPTEMBER 15th

COLUMBIA BROADCASTING THEATER NO. 1—242 WEST 45TH STREET

9:30 Session on MUSIC AND SCIENCE—Dayton C. Miller (Case School of Applied Science), presiding
Otto Ortmann (Peabody Conservatory, Baltimore)—The Psychology of Tone Quality
Glen Haydon (University of North Carolina)—Alfred Day and the Theory of Harmony
Manfred Bukofzer (New York)—The Evolution of Javanese Tone-Systems
Davidson Taylor (Columbia Broadcasting System)—Music Composed for Radio
Dayton C. Miller—Tone Color with Phonodeik Demonstration
(*Discussion at discretion of the chairman*)

MUSEUM OF MODERN ART, 11 WEST 53RD STREET

1:00 Luncheon on Terrace (Reservations must be made in advance with Assistant Secretary Angell or Chase)

2:15 Listen to Broadcast by Sir James Jeans from London

2:30 Film Library Moving Pictures of particular musical interest

MUSIC & ART HIGH SCHOOL, CONVENT AVENUE & 135TH STREET

(*Take Broadway I. R. T. Subway to 137th St.*)

4:00 Instrumental and Vocal Demonstration of Student Work

1939 Musicological Congress, New York: Program *(cont.)*

AMERICAN ACADEMY OF ARTS & LETTERS,
633 WEST 155TH STREET
(Take Broadway I. R. T. Subway to 157th Street or Fifth Avenue Bus No. 4, No. 5 or No. 19)
Contains works and memorabilia of members of the Academy and the National Institute of Arts & Letters.

7:00 Buffet Supper (Reservations must be made in advance with Assistant Secretary Angell or Chase)

AUDITORIUM OF THE AMERICAN ACADEMY OF ARTS & LETTERS,
632 WEST 156TH STREET

8:30 A Concert of Hispanic Music Illustrating the Musical Culture of Colonial and Contemporary Latin America, Francisco Curt Lange presiding

SATURDAY, SEPTEMBER 16th

BEETHOVEN ASSOCIATION CLUB-ROOMS,
30 WEST 56TH STREET
9:30 Hispanic Session, Gilbert Chase (New York, N. Y.), presiding
Francisco Curt Lange (Uruguay) —Americanismo musical
Alfredo San Malo (Panama) and Nicholas Slonimsky (Boston) — Three Piezas by Domingo Santa Cruz and a Danza by Guillermo Uribe Holguin
Juan Lecuna (Venezuela) —Venezuelan Folk Lore (Illustrated at the Piano)
Eduardo Sánchez de Fuentes (Cuba) and Gonzalo Ruig (Cuba) —Subjects to be announced.
H. Burle Marx (Brazil) —A Few Practical Music Problems in Latin America
(Discussion at discretion of the chairman)
1:00 Luncheon (Reservations must be made in advance with Assistant Secretary Angell or Chase)

AUDITORIUM OF THE METROPOLITAN MUSEUM OF ART, FIFTH AVENUE & 82ND STREET
(Take Fifth Avenue Bus No. 1, 2, 3, or 4)
4:00 Concert of 18th- and 19th-Century American Chamber Music, by RALPH KIRKPATRICK and assisting artists: J. F. Peter, String Quartet; J. C. Moller, String Quartet; Raynor Taylor, 'Cello Sonata; Alexander Reinagle,

9

Songs; James Hewitt, "Battle of Trenton"; Benjamin Carr, Songs; Gaetano Franceschini, Trio Sonata

WINDSOR THEATER, 48TH STREET,
EAST OF BROADWAY
8:40 Broadway Musical Comedy: PINS AND NEEDLES. (Reservations must be obtained in advance from Assistant Secretary Angell or Chase; admission, 55 cents to $1.65)
After performance: Assemble outside theater for Visit to Harlem under the chaperonage of Wilder Hobson (For those who can take it)

* * *

SUNDAY AND MONDAY, SEPTEMBER 17th and 18th

LEAVE FOR WASHINGTON SUNDAY AFTERNOON. VISIT THE LIBRARY OF CONGRESS ON MONDAY.
Reservations for the trip must be made in advance

PRICES OF MEALS

Sept. 11	Luncheon	Beethoven Association	$1.00
	Supper	Brazilian Pavilion	2.00
Sept. 12	Luncheon	Rainbow Room Lounge	1.75
	Supper	Fraunces' Tavern	
Sept. 13	Supper	Beethoven Association	1.00
Sept. 14	Luncheon	Faculty Club, Columbia University	
		(extended by the University; limited to 50)	
	Supper	Claremont Inn	1.50
Sept. 15	Luncheon	Museum of Modern Art	1.00
	Supper	American Academy of Arts & Letters	1.50
Sept. 16	Luncheon	Beethoven Association	1.00

Attendance at the series of Sessions and Concerts is free to Members and Delegates. A ticket, costing $1.00, obtainable upon application from the Secretary, 30 East 56th Street, will admit visitors (including wives or husbands of members) to the series.

A New York Sightseeing Yacht leaves the Battery every day at 10:30 and 2:30. Fare, $1.50. The trip round Manhattan Island lasts 3 hours. While no organized tour is contemplated by the Society, the trip is strongly recommended.

10

1939 Musicological Congress, New York: Program *(cont.)*

Appendices

Past presidents left to right, **back row:** Lewis Lockwood, Howard Smither, Philip Gossett, Jessie Ann Owens, Peter Burkholder, James Webster, Richard Crawford; **front row:** Colin Slim, Margaret Bent, Wendy Allanbrook, Elaine Sisman, Jane Bernstein, Ellen Rosand, James Haar

Society Officers and Board Members

1935　Otto Kinkeldey, *President;* Charles Seeger, Oliver Strunk, *Vice Presidents*; Gustave Reese, *Secretary;* Paul Henry Lang, *Treasurer;* Jean Beck, Archibald T. Davison, Carl Engel, Carleton Sprague Smith, *Members-at-Large*

1936　Otto Kinkeldey, *President;* Oliver Strunk, George S. Dickinson, *Vice Presidents;* Gustave Reese, *Secretary;* Paul Henry Lang, *Treasurer;* Glen Haydon, Hugo Leichtentritt, Otto Ortmann, Roy D. Welch, *Members-at-Large*

1937　Carl Engel, *President;* George S. Dickinson, Carleton Sprague Smith, *Vice Presidents*; Gustave Reese, *Secretary;* Paul Henry Lang, *Treasurer;* Otto Kinkeldey, M. D. Herter Norton, Waldo S. Pratt, Harold Spivacke, *Members-at-Large*

1938　Carl Engel, *President;* Carleton Sprague Smith, Howard Hanson, *Vice Presidents;* Gustave Reese, *Secretary;* Paul Henry Lang, *Treasurer;* Dayton C. Miller, Otto Ortmann, Albert Riemenschneider, Oliver Strunk, *Members-at-Large*

1939　Carleton Sprague Smith, *President;* Howard Hanson, Dayton C. Miller, *Vice Presidents;* Gustave Reese, *Secretary;* Paul Henry Lang, *Treasurer;* Otto E. Albrecht, Charles Warren Fox, Curt Sachs, Edward N. Waters, *Members-at-Large*

1940　Carleton Sprague Smith, *President;* Dayton C. Miller, Harold Spivacke, *Vice Presidents;* Gustave Reese, *Secretary;* Paul Henry Lang, *Treasurer;* Warren D. Allen, Alfred Einstein, Carl Engel, Otto Kinkeldey, *Members-at-Large*

1941　Otto Kinkeldey, *President;* Harold Spivacke, George S. Dickinson, *Vice Presidents;* Gustave Reese, *Secretary;* Paul Henry Lang, *Treasurer;* Theodore M. Finney, Glen Haydon, Albert Riemenschneider, Helen M. Roberts, *Members-at-Large*

1942　Otto Kinkeldey, *President;* George S. Dickinson, Warren D. Allen, *Vice Presidents;* Gustave Reese, *Secretary;* Paul Henry Lang, *Treasurer;* Manfred F. Bukofzer, Helen E. Bush, Jacob M. Coopersmith, Ross Lee Finney, *Members-at-Large*

1943   Glen Haydon, *President;* Warren D. Allen, Carl Engel, *Vice Presidents;* Gustave Reese, *Secretary;* Paul Henry Lang, *Treasurer;* Gilbert Chase, Paul R. Farnsworth, Albert Riemenschneider, Curt Sachs, *Members-at-Large*

1944   Glen Haydon, *President;* Carl Engel (d. May 6, 1944), Philip Greeley Clapp, *Vice Presidents;* Gustave Reese, *Secretary;* Paul Henry Lang, *Treasurer;* Manfred F. Bukofzer, Donald J. Grout, Charles Seeger, Edward N. Waters, *Members-at-Large*

1945   Charles Seeger, *President;* Philip Greeley Clapp, Alfred Einstein, *Vice Presidents;* Gustave Reese, *Secretary;* Paul Henry Lang, *Treasurer;* Otto E. Albrecht, Richard S. Angell, Glen Haydon, Richard S. Hill, *Members-at-Large*

1946   Charles Seeger, *President;* Alfred Einstein, George S. Dickinson, *Vice Presidents;* Gustave Reese, *Secretary;* Paul Henry Lang, *Treasurer;* Helen Hewitt, Walter Rubsamen, Otto Kinkeldey, Oliver Strunk, *Members-at-Large*

1947   George S. Dickinson, *President;* W. Raymond Kendall, Gustave Reese, *Vice Presidents;* Edward N. Waters, *Secretary;* Paul Henry Lang, *Treasurer;* Lowell P. Beveridge, Hans T. David, Karl Geiringer, Richard S. Hill, *Members-at-Large*

1948   George S. Dickinson, *President;* Gustave Reese, Paul Henry Lang, *Vice Presidents;* Edward N. Waters, *Secretary;* W. Raymond Kendall, *Treasurer;* J. Murray Barbour, Manfred F. Bukofzer, William S. Newman, George B. Weston, *Members-at-Large*

1949   Curt Sachs, *President;* Paul Henry Lang, Gustave Reese, *Vice Presidents;* William J. Mitchell, *Secretary;* W. Raymond Kendall, *Treasurer;* Richard S. Angell, Manfred F. Bukofzer, George S. Dickinson, Donald J. Grout, Richard S. Hill, Otto Kinkeldey, Charles Seeger, *Members-at-Large*

1950   Curt Sachs, *President;* Gustave Reese, Richard S. Hill, *Vice Presidents;* William J. Mitchell, *Secretary;* Jacob M. Coopersmith, *Treasurer;* George S. Dickinson, Alfred Einstein, Donald J. Grout, Helen Hewitt, W. Raymond Kendall, Paul Henry Lang, Edward N. Waters, *Members-at-Large*

1951   Gustave Reese, *President;* Richard S. Hill, Charles Warren Fox, *Vice Presidents;* William J. Mitchell, *Secretary;* Jacob M. Coopersmith, *Treasurer;* Putnam Aldrich, Willi Apel, Glen Haydon, Otto Kinkeldey, Arthur Mendel, Curt Sachs, G. Wallace Woodworth, *Members-at-Large*

1952   Gustave Reese, *President;* Charles Warren Fox, Otto Gombosi, *Vice Presidents;* William J. Mitchell, *Secretary;* Jacob M. Coopersmith,

Treasurer; Manfred F. Bukofzer, Hans T. David, Helen Hewitt, Richard S. Hill, Arthur Mendel, Curt Sachs, Oliver Strunk, *Members-at-Large*

1953 Donald J. Grout, *President;* Otto Gombosi, Leo Schrade, *Vice Presidents;* Jan LaRue, *Secretary;* Jacob M. Coopersmith, *Treasurer;* J. Murray Barbour, Louise E. Cuyler, Ralph Kirkpatrick, William J. Mitchell, Dragan Plamenac, Gustave Reese, Curt Sachs, *Members-at-Large*

1954 Donald J. Grout, *President;* Leo Schrade, Jacob M. Coopersmith, *Vice Presidents;* Jan LaRue, *Secretary;* Otto E. Albrecht, *Treasurer;* Karl Geiringer, Glen Haydon, Richard S. Hill, Otto Kinkeldey, Gustave Reese, Harold Spivacke, John M. Ward, *Members-at-Large*

1955 Karl Geiringer, *President;* Jacob M. Coopersmith, David D. Boyden, *Vice Presidents;* Louise E. Cuyler, *Secretary;* Otto E. Albrecht, *Treasurer;* J. Murray Barbour, Nathan Broder (elected May 21 to fill unexpired term of Otto Gombosi), Manfred F. Bukofzer (d. Dec. 7, 1955), Hans T. David, Charles Warrren Fox, Otto Gombosi (d. Feb. 17, 1955), Donald J. Grout, Paul A. Pisk, *Members-at-Large*

1956 Karl Geiringer, *President;* David D. Boyden, Dragan Plamenac, *Vice Presidents;* Louise E. Cuyler, *Secretary;* Otto E. Albrecht, *Treasurer;* Jacob M. Coopersmith, Helen Hewitt, Paul Henry Lang, William Lichtenwanger, Gustave Reese, Oliver Strunk, *Members-at-Large*

1957 J. Murray Barbour, *President;* Dragan Plamenac, Nathan Broder, *Vice Presidents;* Louise E. Cuyler, *Secretary;* Otto E. Albrecht, *Treasurer;* Isabel Pope Conant, Karl Geiringer, A. Tillman Merritt, William S. Newman, Curt Sachs, John M. Ward, Emanuel Winternitz, *Members-at-Large*

1958 J. Murray Barbour, *President;* Nathan Broder, Donald J. Grout, *Vice Presidents;* Louise E. Cuyler, *Secretary;* Otto E. Albrecht, *Treasurer;* Willi Apel, David D. Boyden, Karl Geiringer, Glen Haydon, Helen Hewitt, Arthur Mendel, Gustave Reese, *Members-at-Large*

1959 Oliver Strunk, *President;* Donald J. Grout, Gustave Reese, *Vice Presidents;* Louise E. Cuyler, *Secretary;* Otto E. Albrecht, *Treasurer;* J. Murray Barbour, Otto Kinkeldey, Paul Henry Lang, Jan LaRue, William J. Mitchell, Harold Spivacke, John M. Ward, *Members-at-Large*

1960 Oliver Strunk, *President;* Gustave Reese, William J. Mitchell, *Vice Presidents;* Louise E. Cuyler, *Secretary;* Otto E. Albrecht, *Treasurer;* J. Murray Barbour, Henry L. Clarke, Hans T. David, Helen Hewitt, Richard S. Hill, Dragan Plamenac, William G. Waite, *Members-at-Large*

N.B. Otto Kinkeldey served as Honorary President, 1960–1966.

1961 Donald J. Grout, *President;* William J. Mitchell, David D. Boyden, *Vice Presidents;* Louise E. Cuyler, *Secretary;* Otto E. Albrecht, *Treasurer;*

Sylvia W. Kenney, Joseph Kerman, Arthur Mendel, Robert U. Nelson, Claude V. Palisca, Nino Pirrotta, Oliver Strunk, *Members-at-Large*

1962 Donald J. Grout, *President;* David D. Boyden, Arthur Mendel, *Vice Presidents;* Louise E. Cuyler, *Secretary;* Otto E. Albrecht, *Treasurer;* Putnam Aldrich, Hans T. David, Helen Hewitt, Jan LaRue, Carl Parrish, Gustave Reese, Oliver Strunk, *Members-at-Large*

1963 Nathan Broder, *President;* Arthur Mendel, Jan LaRue, *Vice Presidents;* Louise E. Cuyler, *Secretary;* Otto E. Albrecht, *Treasurer;* William W. Austin, Sydney L. Beck, Vincent Duckles, Donald J. Grout, Alfred Mann, Leonard B. Meyer, Emanuel Winternitz, *Members-at-Large*

1964 Nathan Broder, *President;* Jan LaRue, Nino Pirrotta, *Vice Presidents;* Louise E. Cuyler, *Secretary;* Otto E. Albrecht, *Treasurer;* Karl Geiringer, Daniel Heartz, Paul Henry Lang, Claude V. Palisca, Gustave Reese, Milton Steinhardt, *Members-at-Large*

1965 William J. Mitchell, *President;* Nino Pirrotta, Helen Hewitt, *Vice Presidents;* Louise E. Cuyler, *Secretary;* Otto E. Albrecht, *Treasurer;* Nathan Broder, Vincent Duckles, Richard Hoppin, Joseph Kerman, Irving Lowens, Alexander Ringer, Albert Seay, *Members-at-Large*

1966 William J. Mitchell, *President;* Helen Hewitt, Claude V. Palisca, *Vice Presidents;* Louise E. Cuyler, *Secretary;* Otto E. Albrecht, *Treasurer;* Putnam Aldrich, David D. Boyden, Nathan Broder, H. Wiley Hitchcock, Sylvia W. Kenney, William S. Newman, Dragan Plamenac, *Members-at-Large*

1967 Jan LaRue, *President;* Claude V. Palisca, Howard M. Brown, *Vice Presidents;* Louise E. Cuyler, *Secretary;* Otto E. Albrecht, *Treasurer;* Richard L. Crocker, Donald J. Grout, H. Wiley Hitchcock, Imogene Horsley, Sylvia W. Kenney, Edward E. Lowinsky, William J. Mitchell, William S. Newman, Dragan Plamenac, *Members-at-Large*

1968 Jan LaRue, *President;* Howard M. Brown, William S. Newman, *Vice Presidents;* Louise E. Cuyler, *Secretary;* Otto E. Albrecht, *Treasurer;* Richard L. Crocker, Karl Geiringer, Donald J. Grout, Charles Hamm, Imogene Horsley, Kenneth Levy, Edward E. Lowinsky, A. Tillman Merritt, William J. Mitchell, *Members-at-Large*

1969 William S. Newman, *President;* John M. Ward, *Vice President;* Louise E. Cuyler, *Secretary;* Otto E. Albrecht, *Treasurer;* William W. Austin, Vincent Duckles, Karl Geiringer, Charles Hamm, Jan LaRue, Kenneth Levy, A. Tillman Merritt, Nino Pirrotta, *Members-at-Large*

1970 William S. Newman, *President;* Claude V. Palisca, *President-Elect;* John M. Ward, *Vice President;* Louise E. Cuyler, *Secretary;* Otto E. Albrecht,

Society Officers and Board Members

Treasurer; William W. Austin, Vincent Duckles, Helen Hewitt, William J. Mitchell, Nino Pirrotta, Gustave Reese, *Members-at-Large*

1971 Claude V. Palisca, *President;* William S. Newman, *Past President;* Lewis Lockwood, *Vice President;* Louise E. Cuyler, *Secretary;* Alvin H. Johnson, *Treasurer;* Rita Benton, Howard M. Brown, Eugene Helm, Helen Hewitt, William J. Mitchell, Gustave Reese, *Members-at-Large*

1972 Claude V. Palisca, *President;* Charles Hamm, *President-Elect;* Lewis Lockwood, *Vice President;* Rita Benton, *Secretary;* Alvin H. Johnson, *Treasurer;* Howard M. Brown, George J. Buelow, Eugene Helm, Andrew Hughes, Janet Knapp, Martin Picker, *Members-at-Large*

1973 Charles Hamm, *President;* Claude V. Palisca, *Past President;* James Haar, *Vice President;* Rita Benton, *Secretary;* Alvin H. Johnson, *Treasurer;* George J. Buelow, Albert Cohen, Frank A. D'Accone, Andrew Hughes, Janet Knapp, Leon Plantinga, *Members-at-Large*

1974 Charles Hamm, *President;* Janet Knapp, *President-Elect;* James Haar, *Vice President*; Rita Benton, *Secretary;* Alvin H. Johnson, *Treasurer;* Lawrence F. Bernstein, Albert Cohen, Frank A. D'Accone, Robert L. Marshall, Leon Plantinga, Eileen Southern, *Members-at-Large*

1975 Janet Knapp, *President;* Charles Hamm, *Past President;* Daniel Heartz, *Vice President;* Rita Benton, *Secretary;* Alvin H. Johnson, *Treasurer;* Lawrence F. Bernstein, Philip Gossett, Donald J. Grout, Robert L. Marshall, H. Colin Slim, Eileen Southern, *Members-at-Large*

N. B. Gustave Reese served as Honorary President, 1974–1977.

1976 Janet Knapp, *President;* James Haar, *President-Elect;* Daniel Heartz, *Vice President;* Rita Benton, *Secretary;* Alvin H. Johnson, *Treasurer;* Barry S. Brook, Sarah Ann Fuller, Philip Gossett, Donald J. Grout, H. Wiley Hitchcock, H. Colin Slim, *Members-at-Large*

1977 James Haar, *President;* Janet Knapp, *Past President;* Don M. Randel, *Vice President;* Rita Benton, *Secretary;* Alvin H. Johnson, *Treasurer;* Barry S. Brook, Richard Crawford, Sarah Ann Fuller, H. Wiley Hitchcock, Cynthia Adams Hoover, Joseph Kerman, *Members-at-Large*

1978 James Haar, *President;* Howard M. Brown, *President-Elect;* Don M. Randel, *Vice President;* Frank Traficante, *Secretary;* Alvin H. Johnson, *Treasurer;* David D. Boyden, Richard Crawford, Cynthia Adams Hoover, Joseph Kerman, Howard E. Smither, Ruth Steiner, *Members-at-Large*

1979 Howard M. Brown, *President;* James Haar, *Past President;* Richard Crawford, *Vice President;* Frank Traficante, *Secretary;* Alvin H. Johnson,

Treasurer; Margaret Bent, David D. Boyden, William P. Malm, Howard E. Smither, Ruth Steiner, Christoph Wolff, *Members-at-Large*

1980　Howard M. Brown, *President;* Howard E. Smither, *President-Elect;* Richard Crawford, *Vice President;* Frank Traficante, *Secretary;* Alvin H. Johnson, *Treasurer;* Margaret Bent, William P. Malm, Maria Rika Maniates, Leeman L. Perkins, Eugene K. Wolf, Christoph Wolff, *Members-at-Large*

1981　Howard E. Smither, *President;* Howard M. Brown, *Past President;* Joseph Kerman, *Vice President;* Frank Traficante, *Secretary;* Alvin H. Johnson, *Treasurer;* Rebecca A. Baltzer, Maria Rika Maniates, Bruno Nettl, Leeman L. Perkins, Vivian Perlis, Eugene K. Wolf, *Members-at-Large*

1982　Howard E. Smither, *President;* Richard Crawford, *President-Elect;* Joseph Kerman, *Vice President;* Frank Traficante, *Secretary;* Alvin H. Johnson, *Treasurer;* Rebecca A. Baltzer, Lawrence A. Gushee, Anne V. Hallmark, Leonard B. Meyer, Bruno Nettl, Vivian Perlis, *Members-at-Large*

1983　Richard Crawford, *President;* Howard E. Smither, *Past President;* Jan LaRue, *Vice President;* Frank Traficante, *Secretary;* Alvin H. Johnson, *Treasurer;* Lawrence A. Gushee, Anne V. Hallmark, Leonard B. Meyer, Jeremy Noble, James W. Pruett, Bonnie C. Wade, *Members-at-Large*

1984　Richard Crawford, *President;* Margaret Bent, *President-Elect;* Jan LaRue, *Vice President;* Ruth Steiner, *Secretary;* Alvin H. Johnson, *Treasurer;* Jeremy Noble, James W. Pruett, Ellen Rosand, Bonnie C. Wade, James Webster, Craig M. Wright, *Members-at-Large*

1985　Margaret Bent, *President;* Richard Crawford, *Past President;* Robert L. Marshall, *Vice President;* Ruth Steiner, *Secretary;* Alvin H. Johnson, *Treasurer;* Philip Brett, Harold S. Powers, Maynard Solomon, Ellen Rosand, James Webster, Craig M. Wright, *Members-at-Large*

1986　Margaret Bent, *President;* Lewis Lockwood, *President-Elect;* Robert L. Marshall, *Vice President;* Ruth Steiner, *Secretary;* Alvin H. Johnson, *Treasurer;* Philip Brett, Harold S. Powers, Ann Besser Scott, Maynard Solomon, R. Larry Todd, Robert S. Winter, *Members-at-Large*

1987　Lewis Lockwood, *President;* Margaret Bent, *Past President;* Philip Gossett, *Vice President;* Ruth Steiner, *Secretary;* Alvin H. Johnson, *Treasurer;* Jane A. Bernstein, Jane R. Stevens, Richard Taruskin, Ann Besser Scott, R. Larry Todd, Robert S. Winter, *Members-at-Large*

1988　Lewis Lockwood, *President;* H. Colin Slim, *President-Elect;* Philip Gossett, *Vice President;* Ruth Steiner, *Secretary;* Alvin H. Johnson, *Treasurer;* Jane A. Bernstein, Daniel Heartz, Margaret Murata, Jane R. Stevens, Richard Taruskin, Leo Treitler, *Members-at-Large*

Society Officers and Board Members

1989   H. Colin Slim, *President;* Lewis Lockwood, *Past President;* Rebecca A. Baltzer, *Vice President;* Ruth Steiner, *Secretary;* Alvin H. Johnson, *Treasurer;* Daniel Heartz, Cynthia Adams Hoover, Louise Litterick, Margaret Murata, John H. Roberts, Leo Treitler, *Members-at-Large*

1990   H. Colin Slim, *President;* H. Wiley Hitchcock, *President-Elect;* Rebecca A. Baltzer, *Vice President;* Ruth A. Solie, *Secretary;* Alvin H. Johnson, *Treasurer;* Laurence Dreyfus, Cynthia Adams Hoover, Louise Litterick, Jessie Ann Owens, Alejandro E. Planchart, John H. Roberts, *Members-at-Large*

1991   H. Wiley Hitchcock, *President;* H. Colin Slim, *Past President;* Bonnie C. Wade, *Vice President;* Ruth A. Solie, *Secretary;* Alvin H. Johnson, *Treasurer;* Laurence Dreyfus, Margot Fassler, D. Kern Holoman, Jessie Ann Owens, Alejandro E. Planchart, Gary A. Tomlinson, *Members-at-Large*

1992   H. Wiley Hitchcock, *President;* Ellen Rosand, *President-Elect;* Bonnie C. Wade, *Vice President;* Ruth A. Solie, *Secretary;* Alvin H. Johnson, *Treasurer;* Margot Fassler, Walter M. Frisch, Paula M. Higgins, Kenneth Levy, D. Kern Holoman, Gary A. Tomlinson, *Directors-at-Large*

1993   Ellen Rosand, *President;* H. Wiley Hitchcock, *Past President;* Neal Zaslaw, *Vice President;* Ruth A. Solie, *Secretary;* Alvin H. Johnson, *Treasurer;* J. Peter Burkholder, Walter M. Frisch, Paula M. Higgins, Kenneth Levy, Elaine Sisman, Christoph Wolff, *Directors-at-Large*

1994   Ellen Rosand, *President;* Philip Gossett, *President-Elect;* Neal Zaslaw, *Vice President;* Ruth A. Solie, *Secretary;* Rebecca A. Baltzer, *Treasurer;* J. Peter Burkholder, Ellen T. Harris, Craig A. Monson, Elaine Sisman, Judith Tick, Christoph Wolff, *Directors-at-Large*

1995   Philip Gossett, *President;* Ellen Rosand, *Past President;* Margaret Murata, *Vice President;* Ruth A. Solie, *Secretary;* Rebecca A. Baltzer, *Treasurer;* Thomas A. Bauman, Ellen T. Harris, Ralph P. Locke, Craig A. Monson, Judith Tick, Gretchen A. Wheelock, *Directors-at-Large*

1996   Philip Gossett, *President;* James Webster, *President-Elect;* Margaret Murata, *Vice President;* Jan Herlinger, *Secretary;* Rebecca A. Baltzer, *Treasurer;* Carolyn Abbate, Thomas A. Bauman, Rufus Hallmark, Ralph P. Locke, Anthony Newcomb, Gretchen A. Wheelock, *Directors-at-Large*

1997   James Webster, *President;* Philip Gossett, *Past President;* Jessie Ann Owens, *Vice President;* Jan Herlinger, *Secretary;* Rebecca A. Baltzer, *Treasurer;* Carolyn Abbate, Charles M. Atkinson, Rufus Hallmark, Anthony Newcomb, Christopher A. Reynolds, Susan Youens, *Directors-at-Large*

1998 James Webster, *President;* Ruth A. Solie, *President-Elect;* Jessie Ann Owens, *Vice President;* Jan Herlinger, *Secretary;* Rebecca A. Baltzer, *Treasurer;* Wye J. Allanbrook, Charles M. Atkinson, Jeffrey Kallberg, Christopher A. Reynolds, Anne Walters Robertson, Susan Youens, *Directors-at-Large*

1999 Ruth A. Solie, *President;* James Webster, *Past President;* Gretchen A. Wheelock, *Vice President;* Jan Herlinger, *Secretary;* Rebecca A. Baltzer, *Treasurer;* Wye J. Allanbrook, Ian D. Bent, Jeffrey Kallberg, Richard A. Kramer, Anne Walters Robertson, Josephine R. B. Wright, *Directors-at-Large*

2000 Ruth A. Solie, *President;* Jessie Ann Owens, *President-Elect;* Gretchen A. Wheelock, *Vice President;* Jan Herlinger, *Secretary;* Rebecca A. Baltzer, *Treasurer;* Ian D. Bent, Richard A. Kramer, Robert P. Morgan, Rose Rosengard Subotnik, Mark Tucker (d. Dec. 6, 2000), Josephine R. B. Wright, *Directors-at-Large*

2001 Jessie Ann Owens, *President;* Ruth A. Solie, *Past President;* Elaine Sisman, *Vice President;* Jan Herlinger, *Secretary;* James Ladewig, *Treasurer;* M. Jennifer Bloxam, John Daverio, Robert P. Morgan, Michael Ochs, Rose Rosengard Subotnik, *Directors-at-Large*

2002 Jessie Ann Owens, *President;* Wye J. Allanbrook, *President-Elect;* Elaine Sisman, *Vice President;* Rufus Hallmark, *Secretary;* James Ladewig, *Treasurer;* M. Jennifer Bloxam, Lenore Coral, John Daverio, Timothy McGee, Michael Ochs, Pamela Potter, *Directors-at-Large*

2003 Wye J. Allanbrook, *President* (resigned Jan. 2003); Jessie Ann Owens, *Past President;* J. Peter Burkholder, *Vice President* (*President* from Jan. 2003); Richard A. Kramer, *Vice President* (from Jan. 2003); Rufus Hallmark, *Secretary;* James Ladewig, *Treasurer;* Lenore Coral, Scott DeVeaux, James Hepokoski, Mary Hunter, Timothy McGee, Pamela Potter, *Directors-at-Large*

2004 J. Peter Burkholder, *President;* Elaine Sisman, *President-Elect;* Richard A. Kramer, *Vice President;* Rufus Hallmark, *Secretary;* James Ladewig, *Treasurer;* Scott DeVeaux, Virginia Hancock, James Hepokoski, Mary Hunter, Massimo Ossi, Michael C. Tusa, *Directors-at-Large*

2005 Elaine Sisman, *President;* J. Peter Burkholder, *Past President;* Jeffrey Kallberg, *Vice President;* Rufus Hallmark, *Secretary;* James Ladewig, *Treasurer;* M. Elizabeth C. Bartlet (d. Sept. 11, 2005), Thomas Christensen, Virginia Hancock, Cristle Collins Judd, Honey Meconi (from Sept. 2005), Massimo Ossi, Michael C. Tusa, *Directors-at-Large*

2006 Elaine Sisman, *President;* Charles M. Atkinson, *President-Elect;* Jeffrey Kallberg, *Vice President;* Rufus Hallmark, *Secretary;* James Ladewig,

Treasurer; Mark Evan Bonds, Thomas Christensen, Cristle Collins Judd, Honey Meconi, Carol J. Oja, Pamela F. Starr, *Directors-at-Large*

2007 Charles M. Atkinson, *President;* Elaine Sisman, *Past President;* Walter M. Frisch, *Vice President;* Rufus Hallmark, *Secretary;* James Ladewig, *Treasurer;* Michael Beckerman, Mark Evan Bonds, Tim Carter, Carol J. Oja, Pamela F. Starr, Judith Tick, *Directors-at-Large*

2008 Charles M. Atkinson, *President;* Jane A. Bernstein, *President-Elect;* Walter M. Frisch, *Vice President;* Pamela F. Starr, *Secretary;* James Ladewig, *Treasurer;* Michael Beckerman, Karol Berger, Tim Carter, Suzanne G. Cusick, Patrick Macey, Judith Tick, *Directors-at-Large*

2009 Jane A. Bernstein, *President;* Charles M. Atkinson, *Past President;* Honey Meconi, *Vice President;* Pamela F. Starr, *Secretary;* James Ladewig, *Treasurer;* Joseph Auner, Karol Berger, Marcia J. Citron, Suzanne Cusick, Martha Feldman, Patrick Macey, *Directors-at-Large*

Honorary members left to right, **back row:** Lewis Lockwood, Philip Gossett, Joseph Kerman, Howard Smither, Jessie Ann Owens, James Webster, Leo Treitler, Glenn Watkins, Richard Crawford, Robert Marshall; **front row:** Colin Slim, Maynard Solomon, Wendy Allanbrook, Ellen Rosand, Bathia Churgin, Bruno Nettl, James Haar

Honorary Members

George Herzog (1901–1983)	1962
Ernst C. Krohn (1888–1975)	1970
Charles Seeger (1886–1979)	1970
Willi Apel (1893–1988)	1971
Karl Geiringer (1899–1989)	1971
Donald Jay Grout (1902–1987)	1971
Paul Henry Lang (1901–1991)	1971
Dragan Plamenac (1895–1983)	1971
Gustave Reese (1899–1977)	1971
Oliver Strunk (1901–1980)	1971
Edward Lowinsky (1908–1985)	1975
Arthur Mendel (1905–1979)	1975
Armen Carapetyan (1908–1992)	1979
Otto E. Albrecht (1899–1984)	1980
Nino Pirrotta (1908–1998)	1980
William S. Newman (1912–2000)	1981
Vincent Duckles (1913–1985)	1982
Alvin H. Johnson (1914–2000)	1985
Leonard B. Meyer (1918–2007)	1987
John M. Ward (1917–)	1988
Howard Mayer Brown (1930–1993)	1989
Claude V. Palisca (1921–2001)	1991
Eileen J. Southern (1920–2002)	1991
Charles Hamm (1925–)	1993
Lewis Lockwood (1930–)	1993
H. Wiley Hitchcock (1923–2007)	1994
James Haar (1929–)	1995
Joseph Kerman (1924–)	1995
Bruno Nettl (1930–)	1995
William W. Austin (1920–2000)	1996
Harold S. Powers (1928–2007)	1996
Leo Treitler (1931–)	1996
Barry S. Brook (1918–1997)	1997
Jan LaRue (1918–2004)	1998
Leonard G. Ratner (1916–)	1998

Richard Crawford (1935–)	1999
Maynard Solomon (1930–)	1999
Daniel Heartz (1928–)	2000
Janet Knapp (1922–2010)	2000
H. Colin Slim (1929–)	2001
Robert M. Stevenson (1916–)	2001
Richard L. Crocker (1927–)	2002
Kenneth Levy (1927–)	2002
Robert L. Marshall (1939–)	2003
Howard Smither (1925–)	2003
Philip Gossett (1941–)	2004
Ellen Rosand (1940–)	2004
Ruth A. Solie (1942–)	2005
Glenn Watkins (1927–)	2005
Reinhold Brinkmann (1934–2010)	2006
Frank D'Accone (1931–)	2006
Samuel Floyd (1937–)	2006
David G. Hughes (1926–)	2006
Rebecca A. Baltzer (1940–)	2007
James Webster (1942–)	2007
Wye Jamison Allanbrook (1943–2010)	2008
Jessie Ann Owens (1950–)	2008
Vivian Perlis (1928–)	2008
Lawrence F. Bernstein (1939–)	2009
Anthony Newcomb (1941–)	2009
Rose Rosengard Subotnik (1942–)	2009

Corresponding Members

Guido Adler (1855-1941)	1937
Arnold A. Bake (1899-1963)	1937
Giacomo Benvenuti (1885–1943)	1937
Charles van den Borren (1874–1966)	1937
Edward J. Dent (1876–1957)	1937
Anselm Hughes (1889–1974)	1937
André Pirro (1869–1943)	1937
Percy A. Scholes (1877–1958)	1937
H. J. W. Tillyard (1881–1968)	1937
Luiz Heitor Corrêa de Azevedo (1905–1992)	1942
Kurt Francisco Lange (1903–1997)	1943
Egon Wellesz (1885–1974)	1947
Friedrich Blume (1893–1975)	1952
Suzanne Clercx-Lejeune (1910–1985)	1952
Guido M. Gatti (1892–1973)	1952
Geoffrey Sharp (1914–1974)	1952
Knud Jeppesen (1892–1974)	1970
Geneviève Thibault (1902–1975)	1970
François Lesure (1923–2001)	1979
Gerald Abraham (1904–1988)	1980
Kurt von Fischer (1913–2003)	1980
Frank Harrison (1905–1987)	1981
Jens Peter Larsen (1902–1988)	1981
René Lenaerts (1902–1992)	1981
Dénes R. Bartha (1908–1993)	1982
Ludwig Finscher (1930–)	1982
Claudio Sartori (1913–1994)	1983
Carl Dahlhaus (1928–1989)	1984
László Somfai (1934–)	1986
Alfred Dürr (1918–)	1988
Winton Dean (1916–)	1989
Pierluigi Petrobelli (1932–)	1989
Alan Tyson (1926–2000)	1991
Andrew Porter (1928–)	1993
Ursula Günther (1927–2006)	1994
Stanley Sadie (1930–2005)	1994

Margaret Bent (1940–)	1995
Lorenzo Bianconi (1946–)	1995
Reinhard Strohm (1942–)	1995
Michel Huglo (1921–)	1997
David Fallows (1945–)	1999
Paolo Fabbri (1948–)	2000
Julian Rushton (1941–)	2000
Wulf Arlt (1938–)	2001
Giulio Cattin (1929–)	2001
John Deathridge (1944–)	2002
David Hiley (1947–)	2002
Silke Leopold (1948–)	2003
Margaret Kartomi (1940–)	2004
Bonnie Blackburn (1939–)	2006
Hermann Danuser (1946–)	2006
Don Harrán (1936–)	2006
Bathia Churgin (1928–)	2007
Friedhelm Krummacher (1936–)	2007
Catherine Massip (1946–)	2008
Richard Middleton (1945–)	2008
Jean-Jacques Eigeldinger (1940–)	2009
Eva Rieger (1940–)	2009

Editors-in-Chief of the Journal of the American Musicological Society

Volume	Year	Editor-in-Chief
I	1948	Oliver Strunk
II – IV	1949–1951	Donald J. Grout
V/1	Spring 1952	Otto Kinkeldey, Curt Sachs
V/2–3, VI – IX	Summer 1952–Fall 1956	Charles Warren Fox
X/1, 3	Spring & Fall 1957	Gustave Reese
X/2	Summer 1957	Charles Warren Fox
XI/1	Spring 1958	Charles Warren Fox
XI/2–3	Summer–Fall 1958	William S. Newman
XII/1	Spring 1959	Charles Warren Fox
XII/2–3	Summer–Fall 1959	David G. Hughes
XIII	1960	Charles Seeger
XIV – XVI/1–2	1961–Summer 1963	David G. Hughes
XVI/3 – XIX/1	Fall 1963–Spring 1966	Lewis Lockwood
XIX/2–3 – XXII/1	Summer 1966–Spring 1969	James Haar
XXII/2–3 – XXIV	Summer 1969–Fall 1971	Martin Picker
XXV – XXVII	1972–1974	Don M. Randel
XXVIII – XXX	1975–1977	Lawrence F. Bernstein
XXXI – XXXIII	1978–1980	Nicholas Temperley
XXXIV – XXXVI	1981–1983	Ellen Rosand
XXXVII – XXXIX	1984–1986	John Walter Hill
XL – XLII	1987–1989	Anthony Newcomb
XLIII – XLV	1990–1992	William F. Prizer
XLVI – XLVIII	1993–1995	Richard A. Kramer
XLIX – LI	1996–1998	Paula Higgins
LII – LIV	1999–2001	Thomas S. Grey
LV – LVII	2002–2004	Joseph Auner
LVIII – LX	2005–2007	Bruce Alan Brown
LXI – LXIII	2008–2010	Kate van Orden

Annual Meetings

1st   Philadelphia, Pa., Dec. 28, 1935 (with Music Teachers National Association)
2nd   Chicago, Ill., Dec. 29, 1936 (with MTNA)
3rd   Pittsburgh, Pa., Dec. 29, 1937 (with MTNA)
4th   Washington, D.C., Dec. 29–30, 1938 (with MTNA)
5th   New York, N.Y., Sept. 11–16, 1939, International Congress
6th   Cleveland, Ohio, Dec. 30–31, 1940 (with MTNA)
7th   Minneapolis, Minn., Dec. 29–30, 1941 (with MTNA)
8th   New York, N.Y., Dec. 29, 1942
9th   New York, N.Y., Dec. 28, 1943
10th New York, N.Y., Dec. 27, 1944
11th Detroit, Mich., Feb. 23–24, 1946 (with MTNA)
12th Princeton, N.J., Dec. 28–29, 1946
13th Boston & Cambridge, Mass., Dec. 29–30, 1947 (with MTNA & National Association of Schools of Music)
14th Chicago, Ill., Dec. 28–30, 1948 (with MTNA & Music Library Association)
15th New York, N.Y., Dec. 27–29, 1949 (with Society for Music in the Liberal Arts College)
16th Washington, D.C., Dec. 27–29, 1950 (with College Music Association, MLA & MTNA)
17th Rochester, N.Y., Dec. 27–29, 1951 (with MLA & SMLAC)
18th New Haven, Conn., Dec. 29–31, 1952
19th Chapel Hill, N.C., Dec. 28–30, 1953
20th Ann Arbor, Mich., Dec. 27–29, 1954
21st Princeton, N.J., Dec. 28–30, 1955
22nd Urbana, Ill., Dec. 28–30, 1956
23rd Los Angeles, Calif., Dec. 28–30, 1957
24th Boston, Mass., Dec. 27–30, 1958 (with College Music Society & Society for Ethnomusicology)
25th Chicago, Ill., Dec. 27–30, 1959 (with CMS & SEM)
26th Berkeley & Stanford, Calif., Dec. 27–30, 1960 (with CMS & SEM)
27th New York, N.Y., Sept. 5–11, 1961 (with International Musicological Society)
28th Columbus, Ohio, Dec. 27–29, 1962 (with CMS)
29th Seattle, Wash., Dec. 27–29, 1963 (with CMS)
30th Washington, D.C., Dec. 27–29, 1964
31st Ann Arbor, Mich., Dec. 27–29, 1965 (with CMS)
32nd New Orleans, La., Dec. 27–29, 1966 (with CMS & SEM)
33rd Santa Barbara, Calif., Dec. 27–29, 1967

34th   New Haven, Conn., Dec. 27–29, 1968
35th   St. Louis, Mo., Dec. 27–29, 1969
36th   Toronto, On., Nov. 5–8, 1970 (with CMS)
37th   Chapel Hill, N.C., Nov. 14–17, 1971 (with SEM)
38th   Dallas, Tex., Nov. 2–5, 1972
39th   Chicago, Ill., Nov. 8–11, 1973
40th   Washington, D.C., Oct. 31–Nov. 3, 1974
41st   Los Angeles, Calif., Oct. 30–Nov. 2, 1975
42nd   Washington D.C., Nov. 4–7, 1976
43rd   Berkeley, Calif., Aug. 21–27, 1977 (with IMS)
44th   Minneapolis, Minn., Oct. 19–22, 1978 (with Society for Music Theory)
45th   New York, N.Y., Nov. 1–4, 1979 (with SMT)
46th   Denver, Colo., Nov. 6–9, 1980 (with CMS & SMT)
47th   Boston, Mass., Nov. 12–15, 1981
48th   Ann Arbor, Mich., Nov. 4–7, 1982 (with SMT)
49th   Louisville, Ky., Oct. 27–30, 1983
50th   Philadelphia, Pa., Oct. 25–28, 1984 (with SMT)
51st   Vancouver, B.C., Nov. 7–10, 1985 (with CMS, SEM & SMT)
52nd   Cleveland, Ohio, Nov. 6–9, 1986
53rd   New Orleans, La., Oct. 15–18, 1987 (with Center for Black Music Research & CMS)
54th   Baltimore, Md., Nov. 3–6, 1988 (with SMT)
55th   Austin, Tex., Oct. 26–29, 1989 (with SMT)
56th   Oakland, Calif., Nov. 7–10, 1990 (with SEM & SMT)
57th   Chicago, Ill., Nov. 7–10, 1991
58th   Pittsburgh, Pa., Nov. 5–8, 1992
59th   Montreal, Qc., Nov. 4–7, 1993 (with SMT)
60th   Minneapolis, Minn., Oct. 27–30, 1994
61st   New York, N.Y., Nov. 2–5, 1995 (with CBMR & SMT)
62nd   Baltimore, Md., Nov. 7–10, 1996
63rd   Phoenix, Ariz., Oct. 30–Nov. 2, 1997 (with SMT)
64th   Boston, Mass., Oct. 29–Nov. 1, 1998
65th   Kansas City, Mo., Nov. 4–7, 1999
66th   Toronto, On., Nov. 1–5, 2000 (with 13 other organizations)
67th   Atlanta, Ga., Nov. 15–18, 2001
68th   Columbus, Ohio, Oct. 31–Nov. 3, 2002 (with SMT)
69th   Houston, Tex., Nov. 13–16, 2003
70th   Seattle, Wash., Nov. 11–14, 2004 (with SMT)
71st   Washington, D.C., Oct. 27–30, 2005
72nd   Los Angeles, Calif., Nov. 2–5, 2006 (SMT)
73rd   Quebec City, Qc., Nov. 1–4, 2007
74th   Nashville, TN, Nov. 6–9, 2008 (with SMT)
75th   Philadelphia, Pa., Nov. 12–15, 2009

Winners of Society Awards

The Alfred Einstein Award

The Alfred Einstein Award honors each year a musicological article of exceptional merit by a scholar in the early stages of his or her career who is a citizen or permanent resident of Canada or the United States.

1967 Richard L. Crocker. "The Troping Hypothesis." *Musical Quarterly* 52 (1966): 183–203.

1968 Ursula Kirkendale. "The Ruspoli Documents on Handel." *Journal of the American Musicological Society* 20 (1967): 222–73.

1969 Philip Gossett. "Rossini in Naples: Some Major Works Recovered." *Musical Quarterly* 54 (1968): 316–40.

1970 Lawrence Gushee. "New Sources for the Biography of Johannes de Muris." *Journal of the American Musicological Society* 22 (1969): 3–26.

1971 Lewis Lockwood. "The Autograph of the First Movement of Beethoven's Sonata for Violoncello and Pianoforte, Opus 69." *Music Forum* 2 (1970): 1–109.

1972 Sarah Fuller. "Hidden Polyphony—A Reappraisal." *Journal of the American Musicological Society* 24 (1971): 169–92.

1973 Rebecca A. Baltzer. "Thirteenth-Century Illuminated Miniatures and the Date of the Florence Manuscript." *Journal of the American Musicological Society* 25 (1972): 1–18.

1974 Lawrence F. Bernstein. "*La Courone et fleur des chansons a troys*: A Mirror of the French Chanson in Italy in the Years between Ottaviano Petrucci and Antonio Gardano." *Journal of the American Musicological Society* 26 (1973): 1–68.

1975 Eugene K. Wolf and Jean K. Wolf. "A Newly Identified Complex of Manuscripts from Mannheim." *Journal of the American Musicological Society* 27 (1974): 379–437.

1976 Craig Wright. "Dufay at Cambrai: Discoveries and Revisions." *Journal of the American Musicological Society* 28 (1975): 175–229.

1977	James Webster. "Violoncello and Double Bass in the Chamber Music of Haydn and His Viennese Contemporaries, 1750–1780." *Journal of the American Musicological Society* 29 (1976): 413–38.
1978	Charles M. Atkinson. "The Earliest Agnus Dei Melody and its Tropes." *Journal of the American Musicological Society* 30 (1977): 1–19.
1979	Curtis A. Price. "The Critical Decade for English Music Drama, 1700–1710." *Harvard Library Bulletin* 26 (1978): 38–76.
1980	Richard Taruskin. "Opera and Drama in Russia: The Case of Serov's *Judith*." *Journal of the American Musicological Society* 32 (1979): 74–117.
1981	David A. Bjork. "The Kyrie Trope." *Journal of the American Musicological Society* 33 (1980): 1–41.
1982	Gary A. Tomlinson. "Madrigal, Monody, and Monteverdi's 'via naturale alla immitatione.'" *Journal of the American Musicological Society* 34 (1981): 60–108.
1983	Elaine Sisman. "Small and Expanded Forms: Koch's Model and Haydn's Music." *Musical Quarterly* 68 (1982): 444–75.
1984	Jeffrey Kallberg. "Chopin in the Marketplace: Aspects of the International Music Publishing Industry in the First Half of the Nineteenth Century." *Notes* 39 (1983): 795–824.
1985	R. Peter Jeffery. "The Introduction of Psalmody into the Roman Mass by Pope Celestine I (422–432): Reinterpreting a Passage in the *Liber Pontificalis*." *Archiv für Liturgiewissenschaft* 26 (1984): 147–65.
1986	J. Peter Burkholder. "Johannes Martini and the Imitation Mass of the Late Fifteenth Century." *Journal of the American Musicological Society* 38 (1985): 470–523.
1987	Paula Higgins. "*In Hydraulis* Revisited: New Light on the Career of Antoine Busnois." *Journal of the American Musicological Society* 39 (1986): 36–86.
1988	John Daverio. "Schumann's 'Im Legendenton' and Friedrich Schlegel's *Arabeske*." *19th-Century Music* 11 (1987): 150–63.
1989	Anne Walters Robertson. "*Benedicamus Domino:* The Unwritten Tradition." *Journal of the American Musicological Society* 41 (1988): 1–62.
1990	Michael Long. "Symbol and Ritual in Josquin's *Missa di Dadi*." *Journal of the American Musicological Society* 42 (1989): 1–22.
1991	Anne Maria Busse Berger. "The Myth of *Diminutio per tertium partem*." *Journal of Musicology* 8 (1990): 398–426.

1992   Cliff Eisen. "The Mozarts' Salzburg Copyist: Aspects of Attribution, Chronology, Text and Performance Practice." *Mozart Studies* 1 (1991): 253–307.

1993   Massimo Ossi. "Claudio Monteverdi's *Ordine novo, bello et gustevole*: The Canzonetta as Dramatic Module and Formal Archetype." *Journal of the American Musicological Society* 45 (1992): 216–304.

1994   David Gramit. "Schubert and the Biedermeier: The Aesthetics of Johann Mayrhofer's 'Heliopolis'." *Music and Letters* 74 (1993): 355–82.

1995   Anne C. Shreffler. "'Mein Weg geht jetzt vorüber': The Vocal Origins of Webern's Twelve-Tone Composition." *Journal of the American Musicological Society* 47 (1994): 275–339.

1996   Arved Ashby. "Of *Modell-Typen* and *Reihenformen*: Berg, Schoenberg, F. H. Klein, and the Concept of Row Derivation." *Journal of the American Musicological Society* 48 (1995): 67–105.

Rob C. Wegman. "*Miserere supplicanti Dufay:* The Creation and Transmission of Guillaume Dufay's *Missa Ave regina caelorum*." *Journal of Musicology* 13 (1995): 18–54.

1997   Pamela Potter. "Musicology under Hitler: New Sources in Context." *Journal of the American Musicological Society* 49 (1996): 70–113.

1998   Berthold Hoeckner. "Schumann and Romantic Distance." *Journal of the American Musicological Society* 50 (1997): 55–132.

1999   Simon Morrison. "Skryiabin and the Impossible." *Journal of the American Musicological Society* 51 (1998): 283–330.

2000   Margaret Notley. "Late-Nineteenth-Century Chamber Music and the Cult of the Classical Adagio." *19th-Century Music* 23 (1999): 33–61.

2001   Amy Beal. "Negotiating Cultural Allies: American Music in Darmstadt, 1946–1956." *Journal of the American Musicological Society* 53 (2000): 105–40.

2002   W. Anthony Sheppard. "An Exotic Enemy: Anti-Japanese Musical Propaganda in World War II Hollywood." *Journal of the American Musicological Society* 54 (2001): 303–57.

2003   Elisabeth Le Guin. "'One Says that One Weeps, but One Does Not Weep': Sensible, Grotesque, and Mechanical Embodiments in Boccherini's Chamber Music." *Journal of the American Musicological Society* 55 (2002): 207–54.

2004   Pierpaolo Polzonetti. "Mesmerizing Adultery: *Cosi fan tutte* and the Kornman Scandal." *Cambridge Opera Journal* 14 (2002): 263–96.

2005   Mauro Calcagno. "Signifying Nothing: On the Aesthetics of Pure Voice in Early Venetian Opera." *Journal of Musicology* 20 (2003): 461–97.

2006   Gundula Kreuzer. "Oper im Kirchengewande? Verdi's Requiem and the Anxieties of the Young German Empire." *Journal of the American Musicological Society* 58 (2005): 399–450.

2007   David Rothenberg. "The Marian Symbolism of Spring, ca. 1200–ca. 1500: Two Case Studies." *Journal of the American Musicological Society* 59 (2006): 319–98.

2008   Michael J. Puri. "Dandy, Interrupted: Sublimation, Repression, and Self-Portraiture in Maurice Ravel's *Daphnis et Chloé* (1909–1912)." *Journal of the American Musicological Society* 60 (2007): 317–72.

2009   David Trippett. "*Après une lecture de Liszt:* Virtuosity and *Werktreue* in the 'Dante' Sonata." *19th-Century Music* 32 (2008): 52–93.

The Noah Greenberg Award

The Noah Greenberg Award, established by the Trustees of the New York Pro Musica Antiqua in memory of their founder and first director, is intended as a grant-in-aid to stimulate active cooperation between scholars and performers by recognizing and fostering outstanding contributions to historical performing practices.

1978   Cappella Nova (Richard Taruskin, director)

1979   John Hajdu

1980   Philip Brett
        Ross W. Duffin

1981   Maria Fowler
        Timothy Aarset

1982   Spencer Carroll

1983   Mary Cyr and Frederick Stoltzfus

1984   No award

1985   Boston Renaissance Ensemble
        John Hajdu

1986   Evan Johnson

1987   Peter Urquhart

1988   Robert Hill

1989   Linda Kobler

1990	D.C. Hall's New Concert and Quadrille Band (Peter Bloom, Director) Julianne Baird
1991	Kristin Thelander
1992	Alexander Blachly
1993	Richard G. King
1994	Frederick Gable
1995	Jeannette Sorrell and Apollo's Fire
1996	Louise Stein and Andrew Lawrence King Jeanice Brooks and Daniel Leech-Wilkinson
1997	Kate van Orden and The King's Noyse (David Douglass, Director)
1998	Musicians of the Old Post Road (Daniel Ryan and Suzanne Stumpf, Directors)
1999	Victor Coelho and Il Complesso Barocco (Alan Curtis, Director)
2000	Steven Zohn and The Publick Music (Steven Zohn and Thomas Folan, Directors)
2001	Talisman
2002	Maria I. Rose
2003	Christopher Stembridge
2004	Philip Cave and Sally Dunkley
2005	Catherine Gordon-Seifert, Elisabeth Belgrano, and Stephen Stubbs
2006	Christopher Wolverton and Honey Meconi
2007	Elisabeth Le Guin
2008	Adam Knight Gilbert
2009	Liber: Ensemble for Early Music

The Otto Kinkeldey Award

The Otto Kinkeldey Award honors each year a musicological book of exceptional merit published during the previous year in any language and in any country by a scholar who is past the early stages of his or her career and who is a member of the AMS or a citizen or permanent resident of Canada or the United States.

1967   William W. Austin. *Music in the Twentieth Century*. New York: W. W. Norton, 1966.

1968   Rulan Chao Pian. *Sonq Dynasty Musical Sources and Their Interpretation*. Cambridge, Mass.: Harvard University Press, 1967.

1969   Edward E. Lowinsky. *The Medici Codex of 1518: A Choirbook of Motets Dedicated to Lorenzo de' Medici, Duke of Urbino*. Chicago: University of Chicago Press, 1968.

1970   Nino Pirrotta. *Li Due Orfei: da Poliziano a Monteverdi*. Turin: RAI, 1969.

1971   Daniel Heartz. *Pierre d'Attaingnant, Royal Printer of Music: A Historical Study and Bibliographical Catalogue*. Berkeley: University of California Press, 1970.

   Joseph Kerman. *Ludwig van Beethoven: Autograph Miscellany from circa 1786 to 1799: British Museum Additional Manuscript 29801, ff. 39–162 (The 'Kafka Sketchbook')*. London: British Museum, 1970.

1972   Albert Seay. *Opera Omnia*, by Jacobus Arcadelt. Vol. 2, *Madrigali, Libro Primo*. [Tübingen:] American Institute of Musicology, 1971.

1973   H. Colin Slim. *A Gift of Madrigals and Motets*. Chicago: University of Chicago Press, 1972.

1974   Robert L. Marshall. *The Compositional Process of J. S. Bach: A Study of the Autograph Scores of the Vocal Works*. Princeton: Princeton University Press, 1972.

1975   Vivian Perlis. *Charles Ives Remembered: An Oral History*. New Haven: Yale University Press, 1974.

1976   David P. McKay and Richard Crawford. *William Billings of Boston: Eighteenth-Century Composer*. Princeton: Princeton University Press, 1975.

1977   H. C. Robbins Landon. *Haydn: Chronicle and Works*. Vol. 3, *Haydn in London, 1791–1795*. Bloomington: Indiana University Press, 1976.

1978   Richard L. Crocker. *The Early Medieval Sequence*. Berkeley: University of California Press, 1977.

1979 No award

1980 Leeman L. Perkins and Howard Garey. *The Mellon Chansonnier*. New Haven: Yale University Press, 1979.

Nicholas Temperley. *The Music of the English Parish Church*. Cambridge; New York: Cambridge University Press, 1979.

1981 George Perle. *The Operas of Alban Berg*. Vol., *Wozzeck*. Berkeley: University of California Press, 1980.

1982 Joseph Kerman. *The Masses and Motets of William Byrd*. Berkeley: University of California Press, 1981.

1983 Edwin M. Good. *Giraffes, Black Dragons, and Other Pianos: A Technological History from Cristofori to the Modern Concert Grand*. Palo Alto, Calif.: Stanford University Press, 1982.

1984 Howard Mayer Brown. *A Florentine Chansonnier from the Time of Lorenzo the Magnificent*. Chicago: University of Chicago Press, 1983.

1985 Lewis Lockwood. *Music in Renaissance Ferrara, 1400–1505: The Creation of a Musical Center in the Fifteenth Century*. Cambridge, Mass.: Harvard University Press, 1984.

1986 Douglas Johnson, Alan Tyson and Robert Winter. *The Beethoven Sketchbooks: History, Reconstruction, Inventory*. Berkeley: University of California Press, 1985.

1987 Frederick Neumann. *Ornamentation and Improvisation in Mozart*. Princeton: Princeton University Press, 1986.

1988 Karol Berger. *Music Ficta: Theories of Accidental Inflections in Vocal Polyphony from Marchetto da Padova to Gioseffo Zarlino*. Cambridge; New York: Cambridge University Press, 1987.

Anthony Seeger. *Why Suya Sing: A Musical Anthropology of an Amazonian People*. Cambridge; New York: Cambridge University Press, 1987.

1989 Maynard Solomon. *Beethoven Essays*. Cambridge, Mass.: Harvard University Press, 1988.

1990 Thomas Forrest Kelly. *The Beneventan Chant*. Cambridge; New York: Cambridge University Press, 1989.

Craig Wright. *Music and Ceremony at Notre Dame of Paris, 500–1550*. Cambridge; New York: Cambridge University Press, 1989.

1991 No award

Winners of Society Awards

1992   James Webster. *Haydn's "Farewell" Symphony and the Idea of Classical Style: Through-Composition and Cyclic Integration in His Instrumental Music.* Cambridge; New York: Cambridge University Press, 1991.

1993   Eric Chafe. *Monteverdi's Tonal Language.* New York: Schirmer, 1992.

       Lewis Rowell. *Music and Musical Thought in Early India.* Chicago: University of Chicago Press, 1992.

1994   Margot Fassler. *Gothic Song: Victorine Sequences and Augustinian Reform in Twelfth-Century Paris.* Cambridge; New York: Cambridge University Press, 1993.

1995   Richard A. Kramer. *Distant Cycles: Schubert and the Conceiving of Song.* Chicago: University of Chicago Press, 1994.

1996   Charles Rosen. *The Romantic Generation.* Cambridge, Mass.: Harvard University Press, 1995.

1997   Richard Taruskin. *Stravinsky and the Russian Traditions.* Berkeley: University of California Press, 1996.

       Laurence Dreyfus. *Bach and the Patterns of Invention.* Cambridge, Mass.: Harvard University Press, 1996.

1998   Scott DeVeaux. *The Birth of Bebop: A Social and Musical History.* Berkeley: University of California Press, 1997.

1999   Jane A. Bernstein. *Music Printing in Renaissance Venice: The Scotto Press (1539–1572).* New York: Oxford University Press, 1998.

       John A. Rice. *Antonio Salieri and Viennese Opera.* Chicago: University of Chicago Press, 1998.

2000   Mary Hunter. *The Culture of Opera Buffa in Mozart's Vienna: A Poetics of Entertainment.* Princeton: Princeton University Press, 1999.

       Thomas J. Mathiesen. *Apollo's Lyre: Greek Music and Music Theory in Antiquity and the Middle Ages.* Lincoln: University of Nebraska Press, 1999.

2001   Laurel E. Fay. *Shostakovich: A Life.* Oxford; New York: Oxford University Press, 2000.

       Christoph Wolff. *Johann Sebastian Bach: The Learned Musician.* New York: W. W. Norton, 2000.

2002   Ellen T. Harris. *Handel as Orpheus: Voice and Desire in the Chamber Cantatas.* Cambridge, Mass.: Harvard University Press, 2001.

2003 Anne Walters Robertson. *Guillaume de Machaut and Reims: Context and Meaning in His Musical Works*. Cambridge; New York: Cambridge University Press, 2002.

Finalist: Richard Leppert, ed. *Essays on Music*, by Theodor W. Adorno. Berkeley: University of California Press, 2002.

2004 Daniel Heartz. *Music in European Capitals: The Galant Style, 1720–1780*. New York: W. W. Norton, 2003.

Finalist: Wendy Heller. *Emblems of Eloquence: Opera and Women's Voices in Seventeenth-Century Venice*. Berkeley: University of California Press, 2003.

Finalist: Christopher Reynolds. *Motives for Allusion: Context and Content in Nineteenth-Century Music*. Cambridge, Mass.: Harvard University Press, 2003.

2005 Susan McClary. *Modal Subjectivities: Self-Fashioning in the Italian Madrigal*. Berkeley: University of California Press, 2004.

Finalist: Ruth A. Solie. *Music in Other Words: Victorian Conversations*. Berkeley: University of California Press, 2004.

Finalist: Elijah Wald. *Escaping the Delta: Robert Johnson and the Invention of the Blues*. New York: Amistad Press, 2004.

2006 Richard Taruskin. *The Oxford History of Western Music*. Oxford; New York: Oxford University Press, 2005.

2007 Philip Gossett. *Divas and Scholars: Performing Italian Opera*. Chicago: University of Chicago Press, 2006.

2008 Ellen Rosand. *Monteverdi's Last Operas: A Venetian Trilogy*. Berkeley: University of California Press, 2007.

2009 Michael Long. *Beautiful Monsters: Imagining the Classic in Musical Media*: University of California Press, 2008.

The Lewis Lockwood Award

The Lewis Lockwood Award honors each year a musicological book of exceptional merit published during the previous year in any language and in any country by a scholar in the early stages of his or her career who is a member of the AMS or a citizen or permanent resident of Canada or the United States.

2005	Marc Perlman. *Unplayed Melodies: Javanese Gamelan and the Genesis of Music Theory*. Berkeley: University of California Press, 2004.
2006	Kate van Orden. *Music, Discipline, and Arms in Early Modern France*. Chicago: University of Chicago Press, 2005.
	Finalist: James K. Wright. *Schoenberg, Wittgenstein and the Vienna Circle*. Bern; New York: Peter Lang, 2005.
2007	Susan Boynton. *Shaping a Monastic Identity: Liturgy and History at the Imperial Abbey of Farfa, 1000–1125*. Ithaca: Cornell University Press, 2006.
2008	Alexandra Wilson. *The Puccini Problem: Opera, Nationalism, and Modernity*. Cambridge; New York: Cambridge University Press, 2007.
2009	Vanessa Agnew. *Enlightenment Orpheus: The Power of Music in Other Worlds*. New York: Oxford University Press, 2008.

The Music in American Culture Award

The Music in American Culture Award honors each year a book of exceptional merit that both illuminates some important aspect of the music of the United States and places that music in a rich cultural context. The goal of this award is to recognize the best writing on music in American culture, regardless of the source or intended audience of that writing; hence work by a broad range of authors—including performing musicians, journalists, and music critics, as well as academic scholars—will be considered.

2009	George E. Lewis. *A Power Stronger Than Itself: The AACM and American Experimental Music*, University of Chicago Press.

The Claude V. Palisca Award

The Claude V. Palisca Award honors each year a scholarly edition or translation in the field of musicology published during the previous year in any language and in any country by a scholar who is a member of the AMS or a citizen or permanent resident of Canada or the United States.

2005   Ross W. Duffin. *Shakespeare's Songbook*. New York: W. W. Norton, 2004.

Finalist: Charles Brauner. *Mosè in Egitto*, by Gioacchino Rossini (Edizione critica delle opere, I/24). Pesaro: Fondazione Rossini, 2004.

Finalist: H. Wiley Hitchcock. *129 Songs*, by Charles Ives. Middleton, Wis.: A-R Editions, 2004.

2006   David Lawton. *Macbeth*, by Giuseppe Verdi (Opere, I/10). Chicago: University of Chicago Press, 2005.

Finalist: M. Elizabeth C. Bartlet. *Platée*, by Jean-Philippe Rameau (Opera Omnia, IV/10). Kassel: Bärenreiter, 2005.

2007   Jeffrey Taylor. *Earl "Fatha" Hines, Selected Piano Solos, 1928–1941*. Middleton, Wis.: A-R Editions, 2006.

2008   Jennifer Williams Brown. *La Calisto*, by Francesco Cavalli. Middleton, Wis.: A-R Editions, 2007.

2009   Margaret Bent. *Bologna Q15: the making and remaking of a musical manuscript*, Lucca: LIM Editrice 2009.

The Paul A. Pisk Prize

The Paul A. Prize is awarded annually to a graduate music student for a scholarly paper presented at the Annual Meeting of the AMS.

1991   Mark W. Stahura (University of Chicago). "Refuting the *Ripieno* in Handel's Orchestra"

1992   Luisa Vilar-Paya (University of California, Berkeley). "Schoenberg's Re-Centerings: Pitch Organization and Formal Processes in Early Twelve-Tone Music"

1993   John R. Clevenger (Eastman School of Music). "Achille at the Conservatoire (1872–1884)"

1994   Kelley Harness (University of Illinois at Urbana-Champaign). "*La flora* (1628): A Symbolic Transfer of Power in Early Seventeenth-Century Florence"

Winners of Society Awards

1995	Kate van Orden (University of Chicago). "'Chansons plus ménéstrières que musiciennes': Singing to Timbres in Late Sixteenth-Century France"
1996	Stefano Castelvecchi (University of Chicago). "Sentimental and Anti-Sentimental in Da Ponte's and Mozart's *Le Nozze di Figaro*"
1997	Cormac Newark (Christ Church, Oxford). "'Mille sentiments confus l'agitent': Understanding *La Muette de Portici*"
1998	No award
1999	Hilary Poriss (University of Chicago). "'Making their Way through the World': Italian One-Hit Wonders, 1825–1850"
2000	Gundula Kreuzer (St. Hugh's College, University of Oxford). "'Oper in Kirchengewande': Verdi's Requiem and the Anxiety of the German Nation"
2001	Jennifer Shaw (Stony Brook University). "New Performance Sources and Old Modernist Productions: *Die Jakobsleiter* in the Age of Mechanical Reproduction"
2002	Silvio dos Santos (Brandeis University). "Ascription of Identity: The *Bild* Motif and the Character of Lulu"
2003	Ted Dumitrescu (Universiteit Utrecht). "A Flemish-Italian Gift to the Tudors"
2004	Robert Fallon (University of California, Berkeley). "The Record of Realism in Messiaen's Bird Style"
2005	Paul Berry (Yale University). "'Alte Liebe': Johannes Brahms, Clara Schumann, and the Poetics of Musical Memory"
2006	Jesse Rodin (Harvard University). "'When in Rome . . .': What Josquin Learned in the Sistine Chapel"
2007	Emily Abrams Ansari (University of Western Ontario and Harvard University). "Aaron Copland and Cultural Diplomacy: 'Un-American' Composer Meets Cold War Ambassador"
2008	Kimberly Anne Francis (University of North Carolina at Chapel Hill). "'Il reste encore des questions': Nadia Boulanger and Igor Stravinsky Develop the *Symphonie de Psaumes*"
2009	Rebekah Ahrendt (University of California, Berkeley). "'Allons en paix, rebatir nos maisons': Staging the *réfugié* experience"

The H. Colin Slim Award

The H. Colin Slim Award honors each year a musicological article of exceptional merit, published during the previous year in any language and in any country by a scholar who is past the early stages of her or his career and who is a member of the AMS or a citizen or permanent resident of Canada or the United States.

2005 Jann Pasler. "The Utility of Musical Instruments in the Racial and Colonial Agendas of Late Nineteenth-Century France." *Journal of the Royal Musical Association* 129 (2004): 24–76.

2006 Ralph P. Locke. "Beyond the Exotic: How 'Eastern' is *Aida*?" *Cambridge Opera Journal* 17 (2005): 105–39.

2007 Anne Walters Robertson. "The Savior, the Woman, and the Head of the Dragon in the Caput Masses and Motet." *Journal of the American Musicological Society* 59 (2006): 537–630.

2008 Christopher Reynolds. "*Porgy and Bess*, 'An American Wozzeck.'" *Journal of the Society for American Music* 1 (2007): 1–28.

2009 Rose Rosengard Subotnik. "*Shoddy Equipment for Living?*: Deconstructing the Tin Pan Alley Song," Musicological Identities: *Essays in Honor of Susan McClary* (2008).

The Ruth A. Solie Award

The Ruth A. Solie Award honors each year a collection of musicological essays of exceptional merit published during the preceding calendar year in any language and in any country and edited by a scholar or scholars who are members of the AMS or citizens or permanent residents of Canada or the United States.

2007 Martha Feldman and Bonnie Gordon, eds. *The Courtesan's Arts: Cross-Cultural Perspectives*. New York: Oxford Unversity Press, 2006.

2008 Julie Brown, ed. *Western Music and Race*. Cambridge; New York: Cambridge University Press, 2007.

2009 Tom Beghin and Sander M. Goldberg, eds. *Haydn and the Performance of Rhetoric*; University of Chicago Press, 2008.

The Robert M. Stevenson Award

The Robert M. Stevenson Award recognizes outstanding scholarship in Iberian music, including music composed, performed, created, collected, belonging to, or descended from the musical cultures of Spain, Portugal, and all Latin American areas in which Spanish and Portuguese are spoken. The prize is awarded annually to a book, monograph, edition, or journal article, in English, published by a member of the AMS during the preceding three calendar years.

2004   Carol A. Hess. *Manuel de Falla and Modernism in Spain, 1898–1936*. Chicago: University of Chicago Press, 2002.

2005   Cristina Magaldi. *Music in Imperial Rio de Janeiro : European Culture in a Tropical Milieu*. Lanham: Scarecrow Press, 2004.

2006   Walter Aaron Clark. *Enrique Granados: Poet of the Piano*. Oxford; New York: Oxford University Press, 2004.

2007   Kenneth Kreitner. *The Church Music of Fifteenth-Century Spain*. Woodbridge; Rochester: Boydell & Brewer, 2004.

2008   Tess Knighton and Alvaro Torrente. *Devotional Music in the Iberian World, 1450–1800: The Villancico and Related Genres*. Aldershot; Burlington: Ashgate, 2007.

2009   Lorenzo Candelaria. *The Rosary Cantoral: Ritual and Social Design in a Chantbook from Early Renaissance Toledo*. Boydell & Brewer, University of Rochester Press, 2008.

The Philip Brett Award

The Philip Brett Award, administered by the Lesbian, Gay, Bisexual, Transgender/Transsexual, Queer Study Group (LGBTQ) of the AMS, honors each year exceptional musicological work in the field of gay, lesbian, bisexual, transgender/transsexual studies completed during the previous two academic years in any country and in any language.

1997   Elizabeth Wood. "Decomposition." In *Decomposition: Post-Disciplinary Performance,* edited by Sue-Ellen Case, Philip Brett, and Susan Leigh Foster, 201–13. Bloomington: Indiana University Press, 2000; and "The Lesbian in the Opera: Desire Unmasked in Smyth's *Fantasio* and *Fête Galante*." In *En travesti: Women, Gender Subversion, Opera,* edited by Corinne E. Balckmer and Patricia Juliana Smith, 285–305. New York: Columbia University Press, 1995.

1998	Gillian Rodger. "Male Impersonation on the North American Variety and Vaudeville Stage, 1868–1930." Ph. D. dissertation, University of Pittsburgh, 1998.
1999	Martha Mockus. "Sounding Out: Lesbian Feminism and the Music of Pauline Oliveros." Ph.D. dissertation, University of Minnesota, 1999.
2000	Byron Adams. "The 'Dark Saying' of the Enigma: Homoeroticism and the Elgarian Paradox." *19th-Century Music* 23 (2000): 218–35; and "'No Armpits, Please, We're British': Whitman and English Music, 1884–1936." In *Walt Whitman and Modern Music: War, Desire and the Trials of Nationhood,* edited by Lawrence Kramer, 25–42. New York: Garland, 2000.
2001	Bruce Holsinger. *Music, Body, and Desire in Medieval Culture.* Stanford, Calif.: Stanford University Press, 2001.
2002	Lloyd Whitesell and Sophie Fuller, eds. *Queer Episodes in Music and Modern Identity.* Urbana: University of Illinois Press, 2002.
2003	Boden Sandstrom. *Radical Harmonies.* San Francisco: Woman Vision, 2002.
2004	Ruth Sara Longobardi. "Music as Subtext: Reading between the Lines." Chapter 5 in "Models and Modes of Musical Representation in Benjamin Britten's *Death in Venice:* Musical, Historical, and Ideological Contexts." Ph.D. dissertation, Columbia University, 2004.
2005	Judith Peraino. *Listening to the Sirens: Musical Technologies of Queer Identity from Homer to Hedwig.* Berkeley: University of California Press, 2006.
2006	Nadine Hubbs. *The Queer Composition of America's Sound.* Berkeley: University of California Press, 2004.
2006	Sherry Lee. "*A Florentine Tragedy,* Or Woman as Mirror." *Cambridge Opera Journal* 18 (2006): 33–58.
2007	Suzanne G. Cusick. "Music as Torture, Music as a Weapon." Paper presented at the annual meeting of the American Musicological Society, Los Angeles, November 2–5, 2006; and "Queer Performativity and the Gender Order in the GWOT [Global War on Terror]." Paper presented at the conference "Queer Vibrations," Cornell University, March 30–31, 2007.
2008	George Haggerty, Jenny Doctor, and Susan McClary, eds. *Music and Sexuality in Britten: Selected Essays of Philip Brett.* Berkeley: University of California Press, 2006.

2008   Martin Pénet. "L'expression homosexuelle dans les chansons françaises de l'entre-deux-guerres: Entre derision et ambiguïté." *Revue d'histoire moderne et contemporaine* 53 (2006): 105–27.

2009   Annie Janeiro Randall. *Dusty! Queen of the Postmods.* New York: Oxford University Press, 2008.

2009   Philip Ross Bullock. "Ambiguous Speech and Eloquent Silence: The Queerness of Tchaikovsky's Songs." *19th-Century Music* 32 (2008–09): 94–128.

Research and Travel Grant Recipients

The M. Elizabeth C. Bartlet Fund

The M. Elizabeth C. Bartlet Fund for Research in France provides grants to doctoral students at or graduates of universities in the United States and Canada to conduct doctoral or post-doctoral musicological research in France.

2007   Willa J. Collins, Cornell University

2008   Will Gibbons, University of North Carolina at Chapel Hill
        Jennifer Saltzstein, University of Oklahoma

2009   Sarah Gutsche-Miller, McGill University

The Thomas Hampson Fund

The Thomas Hampson Fund was established in 2009 in honor of the *OPUS* Campaign and by the AMS in recognition of Hampson's outstanding contributions to the field of music as a performer, teacher, and scholar. The fund is dedicated to fostering editions and scholarship on classic song in all its contexts, as well as new and innovative technologies for promoting and understanding classic song via interactive media and the Internet.

The Jan LaRue Travel Fund for Research Travel to Europe

The Jan LaRue Travel Fund is intended to encourage and assist Ph.D. candidates, post-doctoral scholars, independent scholars, and junior faculty to travel to Europe to carry out research. The fund honors the memory of Jan LaRue (1918–2004), a distinguished scholar and AMS member admired for his pioneering work on style analysis, the eighteenth-century symphony, and early computer applications in musicology.

2009   Sarah Williams, University of South Carolina

The Janet Levy Fund

The purpose of the Janet Levy Fund is to support professional travel and research expenses for independent scholars who are members of the AMS.

2005	Melania Bucciarelli
2006	Colleen R. Baade Jenny Doctor
2007	Vera Deak Kara Gardner Peter Poulos
2008	Robert Nosow Bonny Miller
2009	Ronit Seter Monique Ingalls
2010	Tina Fruehauf

The Harold Powers Fund

The Harold Powers World Travel Fund for Research on Music is intended to encourage and assist Ph.D. candidates, post-docs, and junior faculty in all fields of musical scholarship to travel anywhere in the world to carry out the necessary work for their dissertation or other research.

2007	Joshua Walden, Columbia University
2008	Max Katz, University of California, Santa Barbara
2009	Kassandra Hartford, Stony Brook University

The Eugene K. Wolf Fund

The Eugene K. Wolf Travel Fund for European Research is intended to encourage and assist Ph.D. candidates in all fields of musical scholarship to travel to Europe to carry out the necessary work for their dissertation on a topic in European music.

2004	Gregory Bloch, University of California, Berkeley Sarah J. Eyerly, University of California, Davis

2005   Patricia Firca, University of Chicago
       Nathan Martin, McGill University

2006   Amy Brosius, New York University
       Michael Eisenberg, City University of New York

2007   Ewelina Boczkowska, University of California, Los Angeles
       Kimberly A. Francis, University of North Carolina at Chapel Hill
       Loren M. Ludwig, University of Virginia

2008   Adeline Mueller, University of California, Berkeley
       Amber Youell-Fingleton, Columbia University

2009   Rebekah Ahrendt, University of California, Berkeley
       Rachel Mundy, New York University

Fellowship Recipients

Alvin H. Johnson AMS 50 Dissertation Fellowships

AMS 50 Fellowships support completion of a dissertation for a doctorate at a North American university.

1986	David Gramit, Duke University
1987	Donald McLean, University of Toronto James Pritchett, New York University
1988	Steven Krantz, University of Minnesota Thomas Sipe, University of Pennsylvania
1989	Thomas Brothers, University of California, Berkeley Bridget Conrad, City University of New York Steven Saunders, University of Pittsburgh
1990	Susan Jackson, City University of New York Ray Komow, Brandeis University Michael Schiano, Brandeis University Amy Stillman, Harvard University Alicyn Warren, Princeton University
1991	David Cannata, New York University Robert Fink, University of California, Berkeley Robert Grimes, University of Pittsburgh Elizabeth Hudson, Cornell University Kristin Knittel, Princeton University bruce mcclung, Eastman School of Music
1992	Dexter Edge, University of Southern California Edmund Goehring, Columbia University Anne MacNeil, University of Chicago Alison Terbell, Princeton University Richard Will, Cornell University

1993 Daniel Beller-McKenna, Harvard University
      Wendy Heller, Brandeis University
      Berthold Hoeckner, Cornell University
      Peter Hoyt, University of Pennsylvania
      Joseph Lubben, Brandeis University
      Mary Ann Smart, Cornell University

1994 Arved Ashby, Yale University
      Stefano Castelvecchi, University of Chicago
      John Clevenger, University of Rochester
      Gayle Clark Kirkwood, University of Pittsburgh
      Benjamin Korstvedt, University of Pennsylvania

1995 Gregory Barnett, Princeton University
      Geoffrey Burgess, Cornell University
      Nancy Guy, University of Pittsburgh
      Heather Hadlock, Princeton University
      John Andrew Johnson, Harvard University
      Stefano Mengozzi, University of Chicago

1996 Todd Borgerding, University of Michigan
      Mary Davis, Harvard University
      Susan Boynton, Brandeis University
      Simon Morrison, Princeton University
      David Schneider, University of California, Berkeley
      Albin Zak, City University of New York

1997 Maribeth Clark, University of Pennsylvania
      Bernardo Illari, University of Chicago
      Gillian Rodger, University of Pittsburgh
      Leslie Sprout, University of California, Berkeley
      Marica Tacconi, Yale University

1998 Theo Cateforis, State University of New York, Stony Brook
      Danielle Fosler-Lussier, University of California, Berkeley
      Dana Gooley, Princeton University
      Beth Anne Lee-De Amici, University of Pennsylvania
      Klara Moricz, University of California, Berkeley
      Rebecca Wagner Oettinger, University of Wisconsin-Madison
      Emanuele Senici, Cornell University
      Rose Theresa, University of Pennsylvania

1999 Lisa Barg, State University of New York, Stony Brook
      Elizabeth Bergman Crist, Yale University
      Giuseppe Gerbino, Duke University
      Barbara Milewski, Princeton University

Martin Scherzinger, Columbia University
Anya Suschitzsky, University of California, Berkeley

2000　Beth Levy, University of California, Berkeley
Susan Lewis, Princeton University
Rebecca Maloy, University of Cincinnati
Ivan Raykoff, University of California, San Diego
Elizabeth Wells, Eastman School of Music

2001　Joanna Demers, Princeton University
Matthew Gelbart, University of California, Berkeley
Nalini Ghuman Gwynne, University of California, Berkeley
Olga Haldey, Ohio State University
Sherry D. Lee, University of British Columbia
Stephanie Tcharos, Princeton University

2002　Patrick Burke, University of Wisconsin-Madison
Julie McQuinn, Northwestern University
Pierpaolo Polzonetti, Cornell University
Holly Watkins, University of California, Berkeley

2003　Melina Esse, University of California, Berkeley
Charles Hiroshi Garrett, University of California, Los Angeles
Roger Moseley, University of California, Berkeley
Scott Paulin, Princeton University

2004　S. Andrew Granade, University of Illinois at Urbana-Champaign
Yossi Maurey, University of Chicago
Kiri Miller, Harvard University
Heather Wiebe, University of California, Berkeley

2005　Emily Iuliano Dolan, Cornell University
David C. Paul, University of California, Berkeley
Benjamin Adam Steege, Harvard University

2006　Marisa Biaggi, Princeton University
Todd R. Decker, University of Michigan
Margaret Martin, Stony Brook University
Lisa Musca, University of California, Los Angeles
Jesse Rodin, Harvard University

2007　Michael Alan Anderson, University of Chicago
Brigid Cohen, Harvard University
Nikos Pappas, University of Kentucky
Noel Verzosa, University of California, Berkeley

2008 Esther Criscuola de Laix, University of California, Berkeley
      Karen Hiles, Columbia University
      Arman Schwartz, University of California, Berkeley
      Daniil Zavlunov, Princeton University

2009 Corbett Bazler, Columbia University
      Martin Nedbal, Eastman School of Music, University of Rochester
      Andrew Oster, Princeton University
      Anna Zayaruznaya, Harvard University

The Howard Mayer Brown Fellowship

Intended to increase the presence of minority scholars and teachers in musicology, the Howard Mayer Brown Fellowship supports one year of graduate work for a student at a North American University who is a member of a group historically underrepresented in the discipline, including, in the U.S., African Americans, Native Americans, Hispanic Americans, and Asian Americans, and, in Canada, visible minorities.

1995 Bernardo Illari, University of Chicago

1997 Maya Gibson, University of Wisconsin-Madison

1999 Georgiary McElveen, Duke University

2001 Mark Burford, Columbia University

2002 Charles Hiroshi Garrett, University of California, Los Angeles

2004 Christina Sunardi, University of California, Berkeley

2005 Hedy Law, University of Chicago

2006 Charles Carson, University of Pennsylvania

2007 Valerie Dickerson, University of California, Los Angeles

2008 Ryan Bañagale, Harvard University

2009 Erika Honisch, University of Chicago
      Sumitra Ranganathan, University of California, Berkeley

Books and Editions Published by the Society

Johannes Ockeghem. *Collected Works.* Edited by Dragan Plamenac. Vol. 2, *Masses and Mass Sections IX–XVI*. Studies and Documents 1. New York: Published for AMS by Columbia University Press, 1947. Rev. ed., 1966.

John Dunstable. *Complete Works.* Edited by Manfred F. Bukofzer. Studies and Documents 2; Musica Britannica 8. London: Published for the Royal Musical Association and AMS by Stainer and Bell, 1953. 2nd, rev. ed., edited by Margaret Bent, Ian Bent and Brian Trowell, 1970.

Johannes Ockeghem. *Collected Works.* Edited by Dragan Plamenac. Vol. 1, *Masses I–VIII*. 2nd, corrected ed. Studies and Documents 3. New York: AMS, 1959. 3rd, corrected ed., 1966.

Joseph Kerman. *The Elizabethan Madrigal: A Comparative Study.* Studies and Documents 4. New York: AMS, 1962.

Edward R. Reilly. *Quantz and His Versuch: Three Studies.* Studies and Documents 5. New York: AMS, 1971.

Edgar H. Sparks. *The Music of Noel Bauldeweyn.* Studies and Documents 6. New York: AMS, 1972.

William Billings. *The Complete Works of William Billings.* Vol. 2, *The Singing Master's Assistant (1778), Music in Miniature (1779)*. Edited by Hans Nathan; Richard Crawford, editorial consultant. Boston: AMS and the Colonial Society of Massachusetts, 1977.

William Billings. *The Complete Works of William Billings.* Vol. 1, *The New-England Psalm-Singer (1770)*. Edited by Karl Kroeger; Richard Crawford, editorial consultant. Boston: AMS and the Colonial Society of Massachusetts, 1981.

International Musicological Society. *Report of the Twelfth Congress, Berkeley, 1977.* Edited by Daniel Heartz and Bonnie Wade. Kassel: Bärenreiter; Philadelphia: AMS, 1981.

Richard Crawford. *The American Musicological Society, 1934–1984: An Anniversary Essay.* Philadelphia: AMS, 1984.

William Billings. *The Complete Works of William Billings.* Vol. 3, *The Psalm-Singer's Amusement (1781), The Suffolk Harmony (1786) and Independent Publications.* Edited by Karl Kroeger; Richard Crawford, editorial consultant. Boston: AMS and the Colonial Society of Massachusetts, 1986.

Essays in Musicology: A Tribute to Alvin Johnson. Edited by Lewis Lockwood and Edward Roesner. Philadelphia: AMS, 1990.

The American Musicological Society: Index to the Papers, Bulletin, and Journal, 1936–1987. Compiled by Marjorie Hassen and Mark Germer. Philadelphia: AMS, 1990.

William Billings. *The Complete Works of William Billings.* Vol. 4, *The Continental Harmony (1794).* Edited by Karl Kroeger; Richard Crawford, editorial consultant. Boston: AMS and the Colonial Society of Massachusetts, 1990.

Johannes Ockeghem. *Collected Works.* Edited by Richard Wexler with Dragan Plamenac. Vol. 3, *Motets and Chansons.* Studies and Documents 7. Philadelphia: AMS, 1992.

Graeme Boone. *Patterns in Play: A Model for Text Setting in the Early French Songs of Guillaume Dufay.* AMS Monographs 1. Lincoln: University of Nebraska Press, 1999.

Lawrence Zbikowski. *Conceptualizing Music: Cognitive Structure, Theory, and Analysis.* AMS Studies 1. Oxford; New York: Oxford University Press, 2002.

Beth L. Glixon and Jonathan E. Glixon. *Inventing the Business of Opera: The Impresario and His World in Seventeenth-Century Venice.* AMS Studies 2. Oxford; New York: Oxford University Press, 2006.

Margaret Notley. *Lateness and Brahms.* AMS Studies 3. Oxford; New York: Oxford University Press, 2007.

Kevin Karnes. *Music, Criticism, and the Challenge of History.* AMS Studies 4. Oxford; New York: Oxford University Press, 2008.

Philip V. Bohlman. *Jewish Music and Modernity.* AMS Studies 5. Oxford; New York: Oxford University Press, 2008.

Charles M. Atkinson. *The Critical Nexus: Tone-System, Mode, and Notation in Early Medieval Music.* AMS Studies 6. Oxford; New York: Oxford University Press, 2009.

Hilary Poriss. *Changing the Score: Arias, Prima Donnas, and the Authority of Performance.* AMS Studies 7. Oxford; New York: Oxford University Press, 2009.

Music of the United States of America (MUSA)

MUSA was established by the American Musicological Society in 1988 as a series of scholarly editions that seeks to reflect the character and shape of American music making. *MUSA*, originally planned to encompass forty volumes, is designed and overseen by the Committee on the Publication of American Music (COPAM), an arm of the Society's Publications Committee. Criteria for determining its contents have been: (1) that the series as a whole reflect breadth and balance among eras, genres, composers, and performance media; (2) that it avoid music already available through other channels, duplicating only where new editions of available music seem essential; and (3) that works in the series be representative, chosen to reflect particular excellence or to represent notable achievements in this country's highly varied music history. All volumes in the series have been published by A-R Editions, Middleton, Wisconsin.

MUSA 1
Ruth Crawford. *Music for Small Orchestra (1926); Suite No. 2 for Four Strings and Piano (1929)*. Edited by Judith Tick and Wayne Schneider. 1993.

MUSA 2
Irving Berlin. *Early Songs, 1907–1914*. Edited by Charles Hamm. 3 vols. 1994.

MUSA 3
Amy Beach. *Quartet for Strings (In One Movement), Opus 89*. Edited by Adrienne Fried Block. 1994.

MUSA 4
Daniel Read. *Collected Works*. Edited by Karl Kroeger. 1995.

MUSA 5
The Music and Scripts of "In Dahomey." Edited by Thomas L. Riis. 1996.

MUSA 6
Timothy Swan. *Psalmody and Secular Songs*. Edited by Nym Cooke. 1997.

MUSA 7
Edward Harrigan and David Braham. *Collected Songs, 1873–1896*. Edited by Jon W. Finson. 2 vols. 1997.

MUSA 8
Lou Harrison. *Selected Keyboard and Chamber Music, 1937–1994*. Edited by Leta E. Miller. 1998.

MUSA 9
Harry Partch. *Barstow: Eight Hitchhiker Inscriptions from a Highway Railing at Barstow, California (1968 Version)*. Edited by Richard Kassel. 2000.

MUSA 10
Thomas Wright "Fats" Waller: Performances in Transcription, 1927–1943. Edited by Paul S. Machlin. 2001.

MUSA 11
Writing American Indian Music: Historic Transcriptions, Notations, and Arrangements. Edited by Victoria Lindsey Levine. 2002.

MUSA 12
Charles Ives. *129 Songs*. Edited by H. Wiley Hitchcock. 2004.

MUSA 13
Leo Ornstein. *Quintette for Piano and String Quartet, Op. 92*. Edited by Denise Von Glahn and Michael Broyles. 2005.

MUSA 14
Dudley Buck. *American Victorian Choral Music*. Edited by N. Lee Orr. 2005.

MUSA 15
Earl "Fatha" Hines. *Selected Piano Solos, 1928–1941*. Edited by Jeffrey Taylor. 2006.

MUSA 16
David Moritz Michael. *Complete Wind Chamber Music*. Edited by Nola Reed Knouse. 2006.

MUSA 17
Charles Hommann. *Surviving Orchestral Music*. Edited by Joanne Swenson-Eldridge. 2007.

MUSA 18
Virgil Thomson and Getrude Stein. *Four Saints in Three Acts*. Edited by H. Wiley Hitchcock and Charles Fussell. 2008.

MUSA 19
Florence Price. *Symphonies Nos. 1 and 3*. Edited by Rae Linda Brown and Wayne Shirley. 2008.

MUSA 20
Songs from "A New Circle of Voices": The Sixteenth Annual Pow-wow at UCLA. Edited by Tara Browner. 2009.